AF587113

HISTORICAL RECORDS

OF THE

BRITISH ARMY.

THE THIRD,

OR

PRINCE OF WALES' REGIMENT OF DRAGOON GUARDS.

ISBN - 978-93-5478-425-5

Design and setting By
Zinc Read
Email- zincread@gmail.com

GENERAL ORDERS.

HORSE-GUARDS,

1*st January*, 1836.

His Majesty has been pleased to command, that, with a view of doing the fullest justice to Regiments, as well as to Individuals who have distinguished themselves by their Bravery in Action with the Enemy, an Account of the Services of every Regiment in the British Army shall be published under the superintendence and direction of the Adjutant-General; and that this Account shall contain the following particulars: *viz.*,

—— The Period and Circumstances of the Original Formation of the Regiment; The Stations at which it has been from time to time employed; The Battles, Sieges, and other Military Operations, in which it has been engaged, particularly specifying any Achievement it may have performed, and the Colours, Trophies, &c., it may have captured from the Enemy.

—— The Names of the Officers and the number of Non-Commissioned Officers and Privates, Killed or Wounded by the Enemy, specifying the Place and Date of the Action.

—— The Names of those Officers, who, in consideration of their Gallant Services and Meritorious Conduct in Engagements with the Enemy, have been distinguished with Titles, Medals, or other Marks of His Majesty's gracious favour.

—— The Names of all such Officers, Non-Commissioned Officers and Privates as may have specially signalized themselves in Action.

And,

—— The Badges and Devices which the Regiment may have been permitted to bear, and the Causes on account of which such Badges or Devices, or any other Marks of Distinction, have been granted.

By Command of the Right Honourable

GENERAL LORD HILL,

Commanding-in-Chief.

JOHN MACDONALD,

Adjutant-General.

PREFACE.

The character and credit of the British Army must chiefly depend upon the zeal and ardour, by which all who enter into its service are animated, and consequently it is of the highest importance that any measure calculated to excite the spirit of emulation, by which alone great and gallant actions are achieved, should be adopted.

Nothing can more fully tend to the accomplishment of this desirable object, than a full display of the noble deeds with which the Military History of our country abounds. To hold forth these bright examples to the imitation of the youthful soldier, and thus to incite him to emulate the meritorious conduct of those who have preceded him in their honourable career, are among the motives that have given rise to the present publication.

The operations of the British Troops are, indeed, announced in the 'London Gazette,' from whence they are transferred into the public prints: the achievements of our armies are thus made known at the time of their occurrence, and receive the tribute of praise and admiration to which they are entitled. On extraordinary occasions, the Houses of Parliament have been in the habit of conferring on the Commanders, and the Officers and Troops acting under their orders, expressions of approbation and of thanks for their skill and bravery, and these testimonials, confirmed by the high honour of their Sovereign's Approbation, constitute the reward which the soldier most highly prizes.

It has not, however, until late years, been the practice (which appears to have long prevailed in some of the Continental armies) for British Regiments to keep regular records of their services and achievements. Hence some difficulty has been experienced in obtaining, particularly from the old Regiments, an authentic account of their origin and subsequent services.

This defect will now be remedied, in consequence of His Majesty having been pleased to command, that every

Regiment shall in future keep a full and ample record of its services at home and abroad.

From the materials thus collected, the country will henceforth derive information as to the difficulties and privations which chequer the career of those who embrace the military profession. In Great Britain, where so large a number of persons are devoted to the active concerns of agriculture, manufactures, and commerce, and where these pursuits have, for so long a period, been undisturbed by the *presence of war*, which few other countries have escaped, comparatively little is known of the vicissitudes of active service, and of the casualties of climate, to which, even during peace, the British Troops are exposed in every part of the globe, with little or no interval of repose.

In their tranquil enjoyment of the blessings which the country derives from the industry and the enterprise of the agriculturist and the trader, its happy inhabitants may be supposed not often to reflect on the perilous duties of the soldier and the sailor,—on their sufferings,—and on the sacrifice of valuable life, by which so many national benefits are obtained and preserved.

The conduct of the British Troops, their valour, and endurance, have shone conspicuously under great and trying difficulties; and their character has been established in Continental warfare by the irresistible spirit with which they have effected debarkations in spite of the most formidable opposition, and by the gallantry and steadiness with which they have maintained their advantages against superior numbers.

In the official Reports made by the respective Commanders, ample justice has generally been done to the gallant exertions of the Corps employed; but the details of their services, and of acts of individual bravery, can only be fully given in the Annals of the various Regiments.

These Records are now preparing for publication, under His Majesty's special authority, by Mr. RICHARD CANNON, Principal Clerk of the Adjutant-General's Office; and while the perusal of them cannot fail to be useful and interesting to military men of every rank, it is considered that they will also afford entertainment and information to the general reader, particularly to those who may have served in the Army, or who have relatives in the Service.

There exists in the breasts of most of those who have served, or are serving, in the Army, an *Esprit du Corps*—an attachment to every thing belonging to their Regiment; to such persons a narrative of the services of their own Corps cannot fail to prove interesting. Authentic accounts of the actions of the great,—the valiant,—the loyal, have always been of paramount interest with a brave and civilised people. Great Britain has produced a race of heroes who, in moments of danger and terror, have stood, "firm as the rocks of their native shore;" and when half the World has been arrayed against them, they have fought the battles of their Country with unshaken fortitude. It is presumed that a record of achievements in war,—victories so complete and surprising, gained by our countrymen,—our brothers—our fellow-citizens in arms,—a record which revives the memory of the brave, and brings their gallant deeds before us, will certainly prove acceptable to the public.

Biographical memoirs of the Colonels and other distinguished Officers, will be introduced in the Records of their respective Regiments, and the Honorary Distinctions which have, from time to time, been conferred upon each Regiment, as testifying the value and importance of its services, will be faithfully set forth.

As a convenient mode of Publication, the Record of each Regiment will be printed in a distinct number, so that when the whole shall be completed, the Parts may be bound up in numerical succession.

INTRODUCTION.

The ancient Armies of England were composed of Horse and Foot; but the feudal troops established by William the Conqueror in 1086, consisted almost entirely of Horse. Under the feudal system, every holder of land amounting to what was termed a "knight's fee," was required to provide a charger, a coat of mail, a helmet, a shield, and a lance, and to serve the Crown a period of forty days in each year at his own expense; and the great landholders had to provide armed men in proportion to the extent of their estates; consequently the ranks of the feudal Cavalry were completed with men of property, and the vassals and tenants of the great barons, who led their dependents to the field in person.

In the succeeding reigns the Cavalry of the Army was composed of Knights (or men at arms) and Hobiliers (or horsemen of inferior degree); and the Infantry of spear and battle-axe men, cross-bowmen, and archers. The Knights wore armour on every part of the body, and their weapons were a lance, a sword, and a small dagger. The Hobiliers were accoutred and armed for the light and less important services of war, and were not considered qualified for a charge in line. Mounted Archers[1] were also introduced, and the English nation eventually became pre-eminent in the use of the bow.

About the time of Queen Mary the appellation of "*Men at Arms*" was changed to that of "*Spears* and *Launces*." The introduction of fire-arms ultimately occasioned the lance to fall into disuse, and the title of the Horsemen of the first degree was changed to "*Cuirassiers*." The Cuirassiers were armed *cap-à-pié*, and their weapons were a sword with a straight narrow blade and sharp point, and a pair of large pistols, called petrenels; and the Hobiliers carried carbines. The Infantry carried pikes, matchlocks, and swords. The introduction of fire-arms occasioned the formation of regiments armed and equipped as infantry, but mounted on small horses for the sake of expedition of movement, and these were styled "*Dragoons*;" a small portion of the military force of the kingdom, however, consisted of this description of troops.

The formation of the present Army commenced after the Restoration in 1660, with the establishment of regular corps of Horse and Foot; the Horsemen were cuirassiers, but only wore armour on the head and body; and the Foot were pikemen and musketeers. The arms which each description of force carried, are described in the following extract from the "Regulations of King Charles II.," dated 5th May, 1663:—

"Each Horseman to have for his defensive armes, back, breast, and pot; and for his offensive armes, a sword, and a case of pistolls, the barrels whereof are not to be und[r]. foorteen inches in length; and each Trooper of Our Guards to have a carbine, besides the aforesaid armes. And the Foote to have each souldier a sword, and each pikeman a pike of 16 foote long and not und[r].; and each musqueteer a musquet, with a collar of bandaliers, the barrels of which musquet to be about foor foote long, and to conteine a bullet, foorteen of which shall weigh a pound weight[2]."

The ranks of the Troops of Horse were at this period composed of men of some property—generally the sons of substantial yeomen: the young men received as recruits provided their own horses,[iv] and they were placed on a rate of pay sufficient to give them a respectable station in society.

On the breaking out of the war with Holland, in the spring of 1672, a Regiment of Dragoons was raised[3]; the Dragoons were placed on a lower rate of pay than the Horse; and the Regiment was armed similar to the Infantry, excepting that a limited number of the men carried halberds instead of pikes, and the others muskets and bayonets; and a few men in each Troop had pistols; as appears by a warrant dated the 2nd of April, 1672, of which the following is an extract:—

"CHARLES R.

"Our will and pleasure is, that a Regiment of Dragoones which we have established and ordered to be raised, in twelve Troopes of fourscore in each beside officers, who are to be under the command of Our most deare and most intirely beloved Cousin Prince Rupert, shall be armed out of Our stoares remaining within Our office of the Ordinance, as followeth; that is to say, three corporalls, two serjeants, the gentlemen at armes, and twelve souldiers of each of the said twelve Troopes, are to have and carry each of them one halbard, and one case of pistolls with holsters; and the rest of the souldiers of the several Troopes aforesaid, are to have and to carry each of them one matchlocke musquet, with a collar of bandaliers, and also to have and to carry one bayonet[4], or great knife. That each lieutenant have and carry one partizan; and that two drums be delivered out for each Troope of the said Regiment[5]."

Several regiments of Horse and Dragoons were raised in the first year of the reign of King James II.; and the horsemen carried a short carbine[6] in addition to the sword and pair of pistols: and in a Regulation dated the 21st of February, 1687, the arms of the Dragoons at that period are commanded to be as follow:—

"The Dragoons to have snaphanse musquets, strapt, with bright barrels of three foote eight inches long, cartouch-boxes, bayonetts, granado pouches, bucketts, and hammer-hatchetts."

After several years' experience, little advantage was found to accrue from having Cavalry Regiments formed almost exclusively for engaging the enemy on foot; and, the Horse having laid aside their armour, the arms and equipment of Horse and Dragoons were so nearly assimilated, that there remained little distinction besides the name and rate of pay. The introduction of improvements into the mounting, arming, and equipment of Dragoons rendered them competent to the performance of every description of service required of Cavalry; and, while the long musket and bayonet were retained, to enable them to act as Infantry, if necessary, they were found to be equally efficient, and of equal value to the nation, as Cavalry, with the Regiments of Horse.

In the several augmentations made to the regular Army after the early part of the reign of Queen Anne, no new Regiments of Horse were raised for permanent service; and in 1746 King George II. reduced three of the old Regiments of Horse to the quality and pay of Dragoons; at the same time, His Majesty gave them the title of First, Second, and Third Regiments of *Dragoon Guards*: and in 1788 the same alteration was made in the remaining four Regiments of Horse, which then became the Fourth, Fifth, Sixth, and Seventh Regiments of *Dragoon Guards*.

At present there are only three Regiments which are styled *Horse* in the British Army,[vii] namely, the two Regiments of Life Guards, and the Royal Regiment of Horse Guards, to whom cuirasses have recently been restored. The other Cavalry Regiments consist of Dragoon Guards, Heavy and Light Dragoons, Hussars, and Lancers; and although the long musket and bayonet have been laid aside by the whole of the Cavalry, and the Regiments are armed and equipped on the principle of the old Horse (excepting the cuirass), they continue to be styled Dragoons.

The old Regiments of Horse formed a highly respectable and efficient portion of the Army, and it is found, on perusing the histories of the various campaigns in which they have been engaged, that they have, on all occasions, maintained a high character for steadiness and discipline, as well as for bravery in action. They were formerly mounted on horses of superior weight and physical power, and few troops could withstand a well-directed charge of the celebrated British Horse. The records of these corps embrace a period of 150 years—a period eventful in history, and abounding in instances of heroism displayed by the British troops when danger has threatened the nation,—a period in which these Regiments have numbered in their ranks men of loyalty, valour, and good conduct, worthy of imitation.

Since the Regiments of Horse were formed into Dragoon Guards, additional improvements have been introduced into the constitution of the several corps; and the superior description of horses now bred in the United Kingdom enables the commanding officers to remount their regiments with such excellent horses, that, whilst sufficient weight has been retained for a powerful charge in line, a lightness has been acquired which renders them available for every description of service incident to modern warfare.

The orderly conduct of these Regiments in quarters has gained the confidence and esteem of the respectable inhabitants of the various parts of the United Kingdom in which they have been stationed; their promptitude and alacrity in attending to the requisitions of the magistrates in periods of excitement, and the temper, patience, and forbearance which they have evinced when subjected to great provocation, insult, and violence from the misguided populace, prove the value of these troops to the Crown, and to the Government of the country, and justify the reliance which is reposed on them.

FOOTNOTES:

[1]In the 14th year of the reign of Edward IV. a small force was established in Ireland by Parliament, consisting of 120 Archers on horseback, 40 Horsemen, and 40 Pages.

[2]Military Papers, State Paper Office.

[3]This Regiment was disbanded after the Peace in 1674.

[4]This appears to be the first introduction of *bayonets* into the English Army.

[5]State Paper Office.

[6]The first issue of carbines to the regular Horse appears to have taken place in 1678; the Life Guards, however, carried carbines from their formation in 1660.—Vide the 'Historical Record of the Life Guards.'

HISTORICAL RECORD

OF THE

THIRD, OR PRINCE OF WALES' REGIMENT

OF

DRAGOON GUARDS.

1685

In the month of June, 1685, when the Duke of Monmouth raised the standard of rebellion in the west of England, many of the nobility and gentry displayed their loyalty by raising forces for the service of their Sovereign; and during the alarm and consternation which prevailed throughout the country, Thomas Earl of Plymouth,—a nobleman highly distinguished for loyalty and attachment to the crown,[7]—a veteran who had fought the battles of his King against the forces of Cromwell,—raised a troop of horse in Worcestershire; another troop was raised by Claudius Earl of Abercorn in Oxfordshire; a third by Henry Lord Eyland at St. Alban's and its vicinity; a fourth by Henry Lord Grey at Dunstable and other towns in Bedfordshire; a fifth by Lionel Walden, Esq., at Huntingdon and its vicinity; and a sixth by Mr. Ambrose Brown in the neighbourhood of Dorking;[8] and, when the decisive battle of Sedgemoor, with the capture and execution of the Duke of Monmouth, had destroyed the hopes of the disaffected, the six troops raised by the above distinguished noblemen and gentlemen were incorporated into a regiment, which ranked as FOURTH HORSE; and the corps thus formed having been continued in the service of the crown until the present time, it is now distinguished by the title of the THIRD, OR PRINCE OF WALES' REGIMENT OF DRAGOON GUARDS, and the various operations in which it has been engaged, with the part it has taken in battles, sieges, and other occurrences, through many eventful periods of history, form the subject of this brief memoir.

The Colonelcy was conferred on the Earl of Plymouth, by commission dated the 15th of July, 1685, and the Lieut.-Colonelcy on Hugh Sunderland, an officer of experience, who had been Major of the Royal Dragoons since 1683. The FOURTH HORSE were armed and equipped as CUIRASSIERS.[9] The men wore hats with broad brims, bound with silver lace, turned up on one side and ornamented with green ribands; scarlet coats lined with green shalloon, and high boots made of jacked leather; they had also scarlet cloaks lined with green, and green horse-furniture embroidered with white, and ornamented with the King's cypher and crown. Their cuirasses were pistol-proof, and they had also iron headpieces called potts. Their weapons were a sword, a pair of pistols, and a short carbine; and, thus equipped, these loyal yeomen had a formidable and warlike appearance. In a few weeks after the regiment was formed, it marched into quarters in Buckinghamshire (viz., to Amersham, Aylesbury, and Marlow), and, having been instructed in the plain and simple exercises practised at that period, it was reviewed on the 20th of August by the King on Hounslow Heath, and again on thc 22nd of that month.

After these reviews the FOURTH HORSE marched into winter quarters at several towns in Gloucestershire; and it is a curious particular in the annals of the regiment, that the first service it was called upon to perform was enforcing obedience to an Act of Parliament which prohibited the cultivation of tobacco. The increased consumption and high price of this article had induced several landholders to cultivate it on their farms, in violation of the law, particularly at Winchcomb and the villages in that neighbourhood. One troop was stationed for a short time at Winchcomb expressly for the purpose of preventing the cultivation of this herb; and when the men left that town the following paragraph appeared in the order for their march: 'Our further will and pleasure is, that you cause parties to be sent, once at least in every week, to our town of Winchcomb and places adjacent, who are hereby ordered to destroy all plants, seeds, and leaves of tobacco which they shall, upon the strictest search, find planted or growing contrary to the Act of Parliament.'[10]

1686

During its stay in Gloucestershire, the first inspection of the regiment was made by Brigadier-General Sir John Lanier, one of the inspecting-generals of cavalry; and the establishment of the regiment, with the rates of pay of each rank, was fixed by a warrant under the sign manual, bearing date the 1st of January, 1686, from which the following is an extract:—

THE EARL OF PLYMOUTH'S REGIMENT OF HORSE

FIELD AND STAFF-OFFICERS.	Per Diem.		
	£.	s.	*d.*
The Colonel, *as Colonel*	0	12	0
Lieutenant-Colonel, *as Lieut.-Colonel*	0	8	0
The Major (*who has no troop*), for himself, horses, and servants	1	0	0
Adjutant	0	5	0
Chaplain	0	6	8
Chirurgeon iv^{s} per day, and j horse to carry his chest, ij^{s} per day	0	6	0
A Kettle-Drummer to the Colonel's troop	0	3	0
	3	0	8

	£	s	d
THE COLONEL'S TROOP.			
The Colonel, *as Captaine*, x^s per day, and ij horses, each at ij^s per day	0	14	0
Lieutenant vi^s, and ij horses, each at ij^s	0	10	0
Cornett v^s, and ij horses, each at ij^s	0	9	0
Quarter-Master iv^s, and i horse, at ij^s	0	6	0
Three Corporals, each at iij^s per day	0	9	0
Two Trumpeters, each at ij^s viii^d	0	5	4
Forty Private Soldiers, each at ij^s vi^d per day	5	0	0
	7	13	4
FIVE TROOPS MORE, of the same numbers, and at the same rates of pay as the Colonel's troop	38	6	8
TOTAL FOR THIS REGIMENT PER DIEM	49	0	8
PER ANNUM	£17,897	3	4

Immediately after the establishment was finally arranged, the FOURTH HORSE were ordered to march into quarters in the metropolis, where they arrived in February, 1686, to assist the Life Guards in the duties of the court; at the same time a detachment of one officer and six men proceeded to Liverpool to convey the specie collected by the officers of the revenue at that port from thence to London; which was probably a very necessary service, as the King, by doubling the strength of his regular army, had made a great increase in his expenditure.

During the summer of this year the regiment was encamped on Hounslow Heath, where it was several times reviewed by the King, and afterwards went into quarters at Cambridge, Huntingdon, and St. Ives.

At this period the following Officers were holding commissions in the regiment:—

Troop.	Captains.	Lieutenants.	Cornets.
1st.	Earl of Plymouth (Col.)	umphry Perott.	ıos. Wendover.
2nd.	Hugh Sunderland (Lt. Col.)	oyley Mitchell.	m. Wentworth.
3rd.	Earl of Abercorn.	enry Holford.	.ncent Martin.
4th.	Henry Lord Eyland.	ɪm. Pendergrast.	m. Fenwick.
5th.	Ambrose Brown.	ıomas Platt.	aniel Vivian.
6th.	Sir Thos. Bludworth.	ɛter Barnsley.	. D. Morton.

Lionel Walden	Major.
Thomas Hodds	Chaplain.
Thomas Platt	Adjutant.
Thomas Jones	Chirurgeon.

1687

In the summer of 1687 the regiment was again quartered for a short time in London, and it was subsequently encamped on Hounslow Heath, where a series of reviews and mock-battles were performed by the troops in presence of the court. The King spent much of his time on the Heath witnessing the exercise of the several corps, and endeavouring to ingratiate himself in the affections of his army, in order to render it subservient in the execution of his designs against the established religion and laws of the country.

Fourth Horse, 1687. Constituted Third Dragoon Guards in 1746.

On the 3rd of November, in this year, the Earl of Plymouth died, and the Colonelcy of the FOURTH HORSE was given to Brigadier-General Sir John Fenwick, who had for several years held the appointment of Lieut.-Colonel of the Second Troop, now Second Regiment, of Life Guards; he was also one of the inspecting generals of cavalry, and was known to be firmly attached to the King, and a zealous supporter of the measures of the court. Several officers resigned their commissions, and they were replaced by men whose principles were presumed to be favourable to papacy and absolute monarchy.

1688

Although the nation was at peace, and arts and manufactures were prospering, yet the minds of the people were troubled, for they saw the King proceeding with rapid progress towards effecting the overthrow of the established religion and laws of the kingdom; while the nobility appeared resolved to make a stand against the arbitrary measures of the court. Thus, the FOURTH HORSE, when they had been only three years in the service of the crown, found themselves in a most perplexing situation; yet their conduct was so truly honourable, that every individual who has served in the corps may reflect with exultation on the fact that, throughout the whole period of its service, its reputation has been preserved untarnished. In the summer of 1688 it again erected its tents on Hounslow Heath; and, several Bishops having been imprisoned and brought to trial for not acquiescing in the King's measures, on the day they were acquitted, his Majesty, after reviewing the army on the Heath, dined in the Earl of Feversham's tent when, on a sudden, the soldiers began to shout and huzza; the King inquired the cause of the noise, and was answered—'Nothing, your Majesty, but the soldiers shouting because the Bishops are acquitted.' The King answered, with evident displeasure, 'Call you that nothing?' and dismissed the troops to their quarters, resolving (according to the historians of that period) never to call them together again until he had remodelled them, by the dismissal of protestants and the introduction of papists. But events were ripe for execution; and the Prince of Orange was, in compliance with the solicitations of the English nobility, preparing an expedition for England to support the established religion and laws.

When the FOURTH HORSE left Hounslow Heath, they proceeded into quarters at Oxford and Woodstock. In the beginning of November they marched to Alresford; and when the Prince of Orange landed at Torbay, they were ordered to advance to Salisbury, where King James's army was assembled; before leaving Alresford, the men, in consequence of an order from the Secretary-at-War, placed their ARMOUR under the charge of the civil authorities of the town, from whence it was subsequently removed to the Tower of London.

King James arrived at Salisbury to command the forces in person, where he again discovered the reluctance of the troops to support the proceedings of the jesuitical faction by which he was governed; and, alarmed by the desertions which took place, he fled to London and ultimately to France. Several corps went over to the Prince of Orange; but the FOURTH HORSE preserved their fidelity to King James until that unhappy monarch forsook the throne; and when the Prince assumed the reins of government, His Highness ordered the regiment to march to Dorking and Ryegate, where it received a draught of 100 men and horses from the Marquis de Miremont's[11] regiment of horse, a newly-raised corps which was ordered to be disbanded.

Sir John Fenwick, adhering to the interest of King James, resigned his commission; and the Colonelcy of the regiment was given to Lord Colchester, from the Lieutenant-Colonelcy of the Fourth Troop of Life Guards, who was one of the first officers that joined the Prince of Orange at Exeter, and took with him several men of his troop.

1689

After the flight of the King, the Roman Catholic soldiers committed some irregularities; and in January, 1689, a squadron of the FOURTH HORSE, with a detachment of Sir George Hewyt's Horse (now Sixth Dragoon Guards), marched to Lewes and Chichester, where they caused three regiments of Irish Roman Catholics[12] to lay down their arms, and afterwards escorted them to Portsmouth; from whence they were removed, under a strong guard, to the Isle of Wight, and were subsequently, sent to Hamburg, and disposed of in the service of the Emperor of Germany.

In the mean time the accession of King William and Queen Mary to the throne was opposed in Scotland, and Viscount Dundee was actively engaged in exciting the northern shires, particularly the Highlanders, to take arms in favour of King James. The FOURTH HORSE, after transferring thirty men and horses to the Blues (which regiment was ordered to proceed to Holland), marched for Scotland, and were placed under the command of Major-General Mackay.

Having arrived at Edinburgh early in April, the FOURTH HORSE formed part of the force employed in the siege of the castle, which the Duke of Gordon held possession of for King James. Shortly afterwards one squadron of the regiment, with two squadrons of the Royal Scots Dragoons (the Greys), and two hundred foot, accompanied Major-General Mackay to the town of Dundee, where two troops of the Royal Scots Dragoons were left, and the remainder proceeded in quest of the rebels.

Major-General Mackay having ascertained that Viscount Dundee had joined Macdonald of Keppoch, who lay before Inverness with a thousand men, determined to confront them with his little band. He crossed the Spey, and advanced to Elgin with all possible speed, and throughout the march he was rejoiced (as he observes in his memoirs) to find his troops animated with the same spirit as himself.

At Elgin the squadron of the FOURTH HORSE halted two days in quarters of refreshment, the men and horses being nearly exhausted. On the third day they proceeded towards Forres, and on the march the General ascertained that Viscount Dundee had taken the road through Badenoch to Lochaber. The squadron then proceeded to Inverness, where Major-General Mackay invited the influential persons in the neighbourhood to meet him to concert measures for opposing the rebels; and, expecting that Viscount Dundee would soon appear with a vast accession of force, several additional corps were ordered from Edinburgh to Inverness. At the same time the remainder of the FOURTH HORSE were also directed to proceed to the same destination.

On the 28th of May the squadron of the regiment at Inverness, with some other troops, in all 640 men, accompanied General Mackay in his advance towards Ruthven Castle, where he expected to meet Colonel Ramsay with 600 Dutch infantry from Edinburgh; but before the general reached the Castle, he ascertained that Ramsay had been intimidated by the threatening aspect of the Athol men, and finding himself in a wild country, to which he was a stranger, surrounded by enemies, he had returned towards Perth: at the same time General Mackay was informed that Viscount Dundee with 2000 hardy mountaineers had arrived that morning at the heights of Badenoch. Under these perplexing circumstances, Mackay turned to the left; then, proceeding down Strathspey, he continued his march for twenty-four hours without a halt; when, having attained a considerable distance in advance of the enemy, he slackened his pace, and was soon afterwards joined by two troops of the Royal Scots Dragoons from the town of Dundee. In the mean time, the enemy followed with all possible expedition, and on their near approach, General Mackay ascertained that several of his officers carried on a secret correspondence with Viscount Dundee, at the same time he had reason to doubt the fidelity of the Scots dragoons. The general, having only the squadron of the FOURTH HORSE and a few Dutch infantry and Scots irregulars on whom he could depend, once more found himself in a perplexing situation; and, not deeming it prudent to march through an hostile country—all papists, with an enemy at his heels four times more numerous than his own little detachment—he commenced his march, at dusk in the evening, by the side of the river, with hungry men and hungry horses, though resolute, particularly the squadron of the FOURTH HORSE, and 200 fusileers, on whom he principally relied.[13] On arriving at Balveny, the troops halted to procure bread for the men and oats for the horses. Having, however, sent out scouts, and none of them returning, General Mackay ordered his party to march forward before the bread was baked, or the horses had eaten a feed of corn, nor halted until four o'clock on the next morning, when neither cavalry nor infantry were able to proceed. However, after two hours' rest, during which time the horses were permitted to feed in a field of corn, he proceeded three miles farther, and took post at the foot of Suy Hill, where he had a view for two miles in every direction in which the enemy could approach. Here the men had some repose, and,[13] their provisions being exhausted, a further supply was sent for from a house in the neighbourhood belonging to the Lord Forbes; but before the food was prepared the general found it necessary to resume his march. On the same day he was joined by Berkeley's (now Fourth) Dragoons, and Leslie's (now Fifteenth) Regiment of Foot. Thus reinforced he resolved to confront the enemy; but the Highlanders, though not inferior in numbers to the King's forces, made a precipitate retreat, and the troops pursued them from the low country until they took refuge in the wilds of Lochaber. The FOURTH HORSE afterwards returned to the lowlands for refreshment, of which they stood in great need: having in this, their first campaign, undergone the greatest fatigues and privation with a constancy and patience, which occasioned General Mackay, who was an officer of much experience, to speak of them in terms of commendation.

The enemy, though compelled to retire, was not to be despised. The lofty, chivalrous spirit of Viscount Dundee rose superior to ordinary difficulties, and he was engaged in arousing the friends of the Stuarts to arms. At the same time General Mackay was at Edinburgh procuring supplies; and, having given directions for a considerable body of troops to assemble at Perth, he proceeded thither without delay. Here he received intelligence of the enemy's increasing numbers, and, although his cavalry had not joined him (excepting two troops of newly-raised horse), he resolved to march forward, with a view of preventing the entry of the Highlanders into the country of Athol. The result was the unfortunate battle of Killicrankie; in narrating which the General observes, in reference to the latter part of the action, '*that if he had had but fifty resolute horse such as* COLCHESTER'S (the FOURTH) *with him, he had certainly, by all human appearance, recovered the day,*'[14] which shows the very high opinion he entertained of the regiment.

Two days after this action, in which Viscount Dundee was killed, and the command of the mountaineers devolved on Brigadier-General Cannon, the FOURTH HORSE joined General Mackay, who proceeded with the reinforcements he received towards *St. Johnston,* to prevent the junction of the disaffected in the shires of Perth and Angus with the rebels, and to keep the latter to the hills. When on this march, a squadron of the regiment highly distinguished itself in an action with a detachment of the enemy, and fully verified the previous commendatory assertions of General Mackay in behalf of the corps. The particulars of this encounter are as follow.

A detachment of rebels, consisting of two troops of horse and about three hundred foot, had seized, at St. Johnston, a quantity of provision, with which they were proceeding to the main body of their army, about seven miles distant;[15] but they were overtaken by Major-General Mackay at the head of a squadron of the FOURTH HORSE and some dragoons, who, regardless of the enemy's numbers, dashed forward with signal intrepidity,—charged and defeated the rebel horse in gallant style,—then rushed upon their foot, and, having broken their ranks, and sabred one hundred and twenty on the spot, the rest were either dispersed or taken prisoners.

This casual encounter produced important results. The enemy, disheartened by the repulse, proceeded towards the north, keeping near the Grampian Hills; and General Mackay with 1400 horse and dragoons marched along the plains at the base of the hills, to restrain the enemy from descending. In this service the FOURTH HORSE were subject to many harassing marches and counter-marches. By day the troops were perpetually in motion; during the night they lay in the fields in a body; and their commander having no confidence in the reports of the country people, who were nearly all hostile to the existing government, he was continually sending out small parties throughout the night to procure intelligence. At length the enemy retreated over the mountains by paths inaccessible to cavalry, and many of the Highlanders proceeded to their homes.

The regiment having sustained considerable loss in this campaign from fatigue and privation, particularly in horses, marched into England to recruit, and was quartered at Warwick and Stratford-upon-Avon.

1690

Having completed its ranks to the numbers borne on the establishment, the regiment marched to the vicinity of the metropolis, and in June, 1690, it furnished a relay of escorts to attend the King to Highlake, in Cheshire, where His Majesty embarked for Ireland, in order to rescue that kingdom from the power of King James. The regiment was subsequently employed in assisting the Life Guards in their attendance on the court; for several months it furnished a daily guard for the Queen-Dowager, at Windsor; and one troop afterwards accompanied Her Majesty to Newmarket.

1691

From the south of England the regiment marched in the spring of 1691 to Lancashire; but it returned to the south in November of the same year, and on the 25th of that month received orders to embark for foreign service.

King William was actively engaged in a war with Louis XIV., who used every means to promote the aggrandizement of France. The FOURTH HORSE formed part of a reinforcement sent to the British army on the Continent; and, after landing at Williamstadt in North Brabant, they marched to Flanders, and went into village cantonments.

1692

On the 23rd of January, 1692, John Lord Berkeley was appointed Colonel of the regiment, in succession to Lord Colchester, who was promoted to the command of the Third Troop of Life Guards.[16]

The FOURTH HORSE were called from their cantonments in the spring of 1692, to engage in active operations; and they formed part of the army commanded by King William in person, which advanced to the relief of Namur, when that fortress was besieged by the French. But on arriving at the banks of the Mehaine, that river was found impassable from heavy rains; the enemy arriving on the opposite bank, the two armies viewed each other across the river, but no action took place; and while the army was thus delayed, Namur fell into the hands of the enemy. The FOURTH HORSE were subsequently engaged in several manœuvres; and they took part in the attack of the French in their position near *Steenkirk*, on the 3rd of August.

On this occasion they formed part of the leading column which, after passing along several narrow defiles and through some woody grounds, deployed on a small plain in front of the enemy, and commenced the attack in gallant style; but not being sustained by the main army, the corps in advance, after gaining considerable advantage and displaying great valour, were obliged to retire. The FOURTH HORSE, after driving back some French squadrons, had advanced to the right skirts of a wood on the left wing, and their gallant bearing, under a heavy fire which thinned the ranks, was conspicuous; but they were eventually forced from their ground by the torrent of superior numbers which came pouring down upon their front. The King ordered a retreat, and the troops performed the difficult operation of retiring through a broken country in presence of an army of superior numbers, in fine order.

After several marches and changes of position, the regiment proceeded to Ghent, where it was joined by a draft of men and horses from the Princess Anne's Horse, commanded by Colonel Francis Langston,—a regiment which, having suffered severely at Steenkirk, was discontinued on the establishment of the army, and the few remaining men and horses were transferred to other corps.[17]

1693

Leaving their cantonments in the spring of 1693, the FOURTH HORSE again took the field, and were with the army in Park camp,—a strong post which covered Louvain, Malines, and Brussels,—and the occupation of this ground enabled King William to defeat the designs of the enemy on Brabant. The FOURTH HORSE were subsequently engaged in several manœuvres, designed to insure the preservation of the bishopric of Liege, and to raise the siege of Huy,—a strong town, pleasantly situated in a valley on the Maese; but this fortress was surrendered while the troops were marching to its relief, and the governor was brought to trial for surrendering it.

The FOURTH HORSE were afterwards encamped near the banks of the Geete, in South Brabant, where the army was attacked by a French force of superior numbers commanded by the Duke of Luxembourg. The regiment was posted on this occasion towards the left of the line, near the village of *Neer-Landen*, to support the infantry in this quarter, and passed the night before the action under arms.

On the 19th of July, as the first rays of morning light glanced upon the hostile armies, the French were discovered in order of battle, and a sudden burst of artillery from the batteries of the allies sent forward a shower of balls, which, rending the ranks of the enemy, formed a prelude to the sanguinary conflict which followed. For some time the fighting was limited to the infantry and artillery, and the FOURTH HORSE were spectators of the fray; yet a cannon shot or two occasionally plunging into the ranks, laid several troopers and their horses dead on the plain. At length the enemy forced the right of the allied army, and routed the Hanoverian and other foreign horse in that quarter, when King William ordered to their aid the British squadrons on the left. Instantly moving from their post, the FOURTH HORSE and other English cavalry gallopped to the scene of conflict, and each squadron charging the moment it arrived, the torrent of battle, which was sweeping the plain, was stayed,—the leading squadrons of the enemy were broken,—and the British horsemen, mixing fiercely in the combat, displayed their native valour and intrepidity. Yet the cavalry and infantry on the right wing, having already quitted the field, the chivalrous horsemen of Britain were unable to resist the superior numbers of the enemy which came pouring down on every side; and they were ordered to retire, a movement which was not executed without some confusion and considerable loss.[18] The French remained masters of the field, but the number of their killed and wounded exceeded that of the allies.[19]

The FOURTH HORSE, having retired from the field of battle by the bridge at Neer-Hespen, proceeded that night to Tirlemont. They were subsequently encamped near Brussels, and after taking part in several manœuvres and skirmishes, they returned to their former station at Ghent.

1694

On the 24th January, 1694, King William conferred the Colonelcy on Lieut.-Colonel Cornelius Wood (an officer of signal merit, who had frequently distinguished himself), from the Seventh Horse, now Sixth Dragoon Guards.

After passing the winter at Ghent, the FOURTH HORSE again took the field in May, 1694, and, after several marches, were encamped with the army on the plain near Mont St. André, where they were reviewed by the King on the 16th of August, in brigade with the regiments of Leveson, Wyndham, and Galway.[20] They passed the summer in manœuvring and skirmishing on the verdant plains of the Netherlands, and on the frontiers of Liege,—performing many long and toilsome marches through a country which, having for several years been the seat of war, was changed from a land of smiling plenty and contentment to a scene of outrage, devastation, and misery. After forming part of the covering army during the siege of *Huy*, which surrendered in September, the FOURTH HORSE marched back to Flanders, and again occupied quarters at Ghent.

1695

In the spring of 1695 thirty men per troop were suddenly called out of quarters to take the field; but after a reconnoissance towards the enemy's frontiers, where they were erecting some extensive lines of defence, the detachment returned to its former quarters. In May the regiment marched out of Ghent, and taking its post in the right wing of the army, encamped at Arseele, was reviewed by the King, with the other English cavalry, on the 31st of that month. In June the regiment was removed from the right to the left wing of the army;[21] and when King William had, by skilful manœuvres, drawn the enemy to the Flanders side of their line of entrenchments, and invested the strong fortress of *Namur*, the FOURTH HORSE formed part of the force detached, under the Earl of Athlone, towards Fleurus, for the convenience of forage, and to observe the enemy on that side. While on this service they were several weeks in comfortable quarters, or moving quietly from village to village,—the horses feeding on the grassy plains of Hainault,—the detached parties patrolling along the front, to observe the motions of the enemy; meanwhile the infantry were encamped between Deynse and Thielt, and the besieging force made rapid progress. At length, owing to some movements of the enemy, the FOURTH HORSE proceeded towards Bruges; they subsequently made several forced marches, and towards the end of July were encamped on the undulating grounds between Genappe and Waterloo. Two powerful armies were at this period manœuvring, and while the French advanced with confidence to raise the siege of *Namur*, the allies interposed to cover the besieging force. In the course of these manœuvres the FOURTH HORSE moved to the vicinity of *Namur*, and after the surrender of the citadel they marched to the neighbourhood of Nivelles, and were subsequently encamped at Halle, from whence they proceeded in the autumn to their former station at Ghent.

1696

During the summer of 1696 the FOURTH HORSE and Wyndham's Regiment (now 6th Dragoon Guards) formed part of the army in Brabant, under King William in person, while the remainder of the British cavalry continued in Flanders. For this purpose the two regiments left Ghent on the 1st of

June, and having joined the main army on the march near Gemblours on the 20th of that month, were reviewed on the 24th by his Majesty, near Corbais. The summer was passed by the FOURTH HORSE in manœuvring, patrolling, and skirmishing on the plains of Brabant, and in performing out-post duty; and, returning to Flanders in the autumn, they once more occupied quarters at Ghent.

1697

The regiment left Flanders in the early part of May, 1697, and, having passed the Scheldt at Dendermond, joined the army encamped at St. Quintin Linneck on the 16th of that month. It took part in the manœuvres of this campaign, and, after several marches, was encamped a short time before Brussels, from whence it was detached, for the convenience of forage, to Wavre; and while at this station hostilities were terminated by the peace of Ryswick, when it was ordered to return to England.

From Wavre the regiment marched to Flanders, from whence it embarked for England, where it arrived in December, and was ordered to march into quarters in Staffordshire; at the same time the establishment was reduced from fifty to thirty-one private men per troop.

1698
1700
1701
1702

During the summer of 1698 it was occupying quarters at Uttoxeter and Penxridge; and in August, of the same year, it was reviewed by the Duke of Schomberg at Lichfield. It remained in Staffordshire until the month of June, 1700, when it proceeded to the vicinity of London, and was reviewed by his Majesty on Hounslow Heath; and in November of the following year, furnished a relay of escorts to attend the King from Margate to London, when his Majesty returned from the continent. It was subsequently stationed in the vicinity of London, and in the beginning of 1702 received orders to hold itself in readiness for foreign service: at the same time the establishment was again augmented to fifty men per troop.

The accession of the Duke of Anjou (grandson of Louis XIV.) to the throne of Spain, in violation of recent treaties, had re-kindled the flame of war in Europe, and King William once more united with the continental states to reduce the exorbitant power of France. In the mean time the Kings of France and Spain proclaimed the Pretender King of Great Britain, by the title of James III. This proceeding made the nation sensible of the latent designs of France; the preparations for war were expedited; and in the beginning of March, 1702, the FOURTH HORSE embarked at Blackwall and Deptford. But the death of King William occurring (8th of March) before the transports sailed, the regiment was ordered to disembark and march into quarters in the villages near London. Queen Anne, however, continued the course of policy adopted by her predecessor, and on the 11th of March the regiment was ordered to re-embark and proceed to Holland, where it arrived towards the end of the same month, and went into cantonments near Breda.

The FOURTH HORSE, with three other regiments of British cavalry and two of infantry,[22] were stationed near Breda, until the 21st of June, when they marched under the orders of Lieut.-General Lumley to join the army. The French attempted to intercept these regiments; but by forced marches they eluded the enemy, and arrived at the camp near Duckenburg, towards the end of the same month.

The French, having obtained possession of the Spanish Netherlands, the campaign commenced on the Dutch frontiers. The FOURTH HORSE, forming part of the army commanded by the Earl of Marlborough, advanced against the immense force of the enemy under the Duke of Burgundy and Marshal Boufflers. Having crossed the Maese near Grave, the British troops were engaged in several daring and skilful manœuvres in North Brabant and the province of Limburg, by which the designs of the enemy were frustrated.

When the allies besieged *Venloo*, the *Fourth Horse* were with the troops employed in observing the enemy, and in protecting the supplies of forage,[25] provision, and ammunition: they were also similarly engaged during the sieges of *Ruremonde* and *Stevenswaert*.

These fortresses having been captured, the regiment quitted its camp at Soutendael about midnight, on the 10th of October, and, having crossed the little river Jaar, advanced with the army towards the city of *Liege*, where it arrived about three in the following morning, when the suburb of St. Walburg was found in flames, the French having, upon the sudden advance of the allies, attempted the destruction of the suburbs by fire, and afterwards retired into the citadel, and into a detached fortress called the *Chartreuse*.

The FOURTH HORSE marched into the city of Liege on the 14th of October, where they remained until the 25th, when they were detached across the river to invest the *Chartreuse*; and, after the surrender of this place, they were employed in escorting the garrison towards Antwerp.[23] Having performed this service they went into village cantonments, and before the following spring the British commander was advanced to the dignity of DUKE of Marlborough.

1703

Having passed the winter in Dutch Brabant, the FOURTH HORSE, moving from their quarters in May, 1703, traversed the country to the vicinity of Maestricht; at the same time one division of the army besieged and took *Bonn*. They were subsequently encamped near the banks of the Maese, where the Duke of Marlborough assembled the army; and on the 24th of May advanced against the enemy, who occupied an advantageous post near Tongres; but on the approach of the allies the French retired, and afterwards took post behind their fortified lines.

The FOURTH HORSE were subsequently encamped with the army near *Haneff*, where they were engaged in a slight skirmish with a detachment of the enemy. The Duke of

Marlborough was desirous of attacking the French lines, but was prevented by the indecision of the Dutch generals and field-deputies. The FOURTH HORSE were also employed in the operations which preceded the investiture of *Huy*, and formed part of the covering army during the siege of that place. They were afterwards in the lines of circumvallation before *Limburg*; and after the surrender of this place they proceeded to Liege; and on the 4th of October joined the camp at St. Trond, where they halted a few days, and were subsequently distributed into cantonments.

1704

The British horse again passed the winter amongst the rude peasantry of Holland, and assembled with the army in the spring of 1704 near Ruremonde, from whence they directed their march to Cologne, and afterwards proceeded through a delightful country to Coblentz, a town situate at the conflux of the Rhine and Moselle. By these movements the Duke of Marlborough indicated a design of carrying on the war in the direction of the Moselle; but he had a more noble and hazardous object in view.

The Elector of Bavaria, who is presumed to have aspired to the imperial dignity, had commenced hostilities against the Emperor of Germany. In 1703, 30,000 French troops marched through the Black Forest to assist him, the united French and Bavarian armies were carrying all before them, and it was apprehended that if something extraordinary was not undertaken, the Elector of Bavaria would gain the imperial throne,—Germany would be subjected to French domination,—and Louis XIV. would dictate laws to Europe. To avert this disaster, the Duke of Marlborough resolved to march the army under his command from the Netherlands into the heart of Germany.

In pursuance of this object, the FOURTH HORSE, having crossed the Rhine and the Moselle, moved forward with the other cavalry regiments in advance of the main army, and commenced their march on an expedition which produced the most stupendous results. During the advance the regiments invariably moved from their camp ground at the first dawn of morning light, completed the march before the heat became oppressive, and passed the remainder of the day in repose, or in preparing for the succeeding day's march.[24]

Continuing their route, under favourable circumstances and in excellent order, the British cavalry arrived towards the end of May at the suburbs of Mentz, in the west of Germany, where they halted a day to rest their horses. From this place they advanced in four days to Ladenburg, in the margraviate of Baden, and having passed the Neckar, halted one day at their camp beyond the town. From thence they directed their march towards the Danube; while the nations of Europe gazed with astonishment at this splendid enterprise, and the different states through which the troops passed hailed their arrival with acclamations. At length a junction was effected between the army of the Duke of Marlborough and the forces of the German empire, and the united troops co-operated in offensive measures.

The FOURTH HORSE, having thus marched from the ocean to the Danube, took an active part in the operations which succeeded; and they formed part of the forces which advanced at three o'clock on the morning of the 2nd of July, and after traversing many miles of difficult country, arrived in front of the enemy's entrenched position on the heights of *Schellenberg*, and commenced the attack about six in the evening.

The infantry having advanced in the face of a storm of fire from the enemy's batteries, and commenced the assault, were forced to give way, when the French and Bavarians, issuing from their works, charged the broken ranks, but were driven back. The attack was renewed with similar results. The infantry, reduced in numbers and exhausted by repeated struggles, were giving way, when Lieutenant-General Lumley led the English horse to their aid, and prevented a repulse. The infantry renewed the attack, and eventually the enemy was driven from the works. At this moment the FOURTH HORSE and other cavalry gallopping forward, by a furious charge completed the victory.[25] The broken battalions and squadrons fled in confusion, pursued by the victorious British and German horsemen, who intercepted the fugitives on every side, and the carnage which followed was dreadful. Many of the French and Bavarians were intercepted on the way to Donawerth, others hurrying to the bridge of boats broke it down by their weight and perished in the river. Their commander, Count D'Arco, escaped with difficulty. Sixteen pieces of cannon, thirteen colours, all the tents, equipages, and a quantity of plate, fell into the hands of the victors. The loss of the regiment was not great;—Adjutant Skelton and several men and horses were killed, and others wounded; and its Colonel, Major-General Wood, was also wounded.[26]

This brilliant success was followed by other offensive operations, in which the FOURTH HORSE took part; but they were not engaged in executing that cruel order, in obedience to which the unfortunate country of Bavaria was enveloped in flames, and above 300 towns, villages, and hamlets were destroyed: this relentless severity was the work of the Germans.[27] At length another reinforcement of French troops arrived, and the united French and Bavarians took post in the valley of the Danube, near the village of *Blenheim*.

About three o'clock on the morning of the 13th of August the allied army advanced, and after traversing several miles of rugged ground, and overcoming many local difficulties, arrived in presence of the enemy; and the FOURTH HORSE, forming part of the cavalry of the left wing under Major-General Wood, had their post in the first line; the right wing being composed of Germans under Prince Eugene of Savoy. About noon the troops, advancing across the little river Nebel, by bridges prepared for the occasion, commenced the engagement, and a succession of attacks were made and resisted with great bravery on both sides. The FOURTH HORSE, with the other English cavalry regiments, were engaged in the early part of the action[28] with the household troops of

France, and the superior spirit and power of the British horsemen were conspicuous, particularly in the unconquerable resolution with which they renewed the attack after a temporary repulse; yet the palm of victory was nobly contested, and the combatants fought hand to hand until the plain was covered with dead. After successive efforts made by the adverse armies—the one to advance, and the other to maintain its ground—the protracted contest drew to a crisis, and the French infantry began to shrink before the tempest of balls which thinned their ranks, while their cavalry, broken and dispirited, gave way, when nine battalions were cut to pieces or made prisoners. The enemy attempted to restore the battle, but the allied horse, once more rushing forward with tremendous force, decided the fate of the day. The enemy, after an irregular fire, fled in dismay, and the regiment which forms the subject of this memoir, after distinguishing itself in the charge, pursued the French squadrons with terrible clamour and confusion in the direction of Sonderheim, smiting them to the ground, and chasing them down the declivity near *Blenheim* into the Danube, where numbers were drowned. At the same time their commander-in-chief, Marshal Tallard, and several other officers and many men, were made prisoners.[29]

While this regiment was pursuing the French horsemen towards the Danube, another part of the army surrounded the village of *Blenheim*, where twelve squadrons of dragoons and twenty-four battalions of infantry were forced to surrender themselves prisoners of war. At the samc time the Germans on the right, under Prince Eugene, were also triumphant. Thus a victory was achieved which shed lustre on the British arms, and the record of these events forms a page in history of which every Englishman may be justly proud, particularly the corps whose valour delivered the empire from impending ruin, and whose fame resounded throughout Christendom.[30]

The FOURTH HORSE had Lieutenant-Colonel Fetherstonhalgh and Cornet Ordairne killed; also Captain Armstrong, Captain Shute, Lieutenant Dove, Cornet

Forester, and Cornet Stevenson, wounded. Of the private men killed and wounded no return appears to have been preserved; but in the War-Office books the regiment is stated to have had forty-seven horses killed in this action.

Having passed the night after the battle on the field, the FOURTH HORSE followed for several days the rear of the defeated army, which repassed the Black Forest, and retired across the Rhine. On the 6th of September the regiment was at Kirlach; it passed the Rhine on the same day to attack some squadrons which appeared on the rising ground near Philipsburg; but, on the advance of the English horsemen, the French retreated across the Queich, and made preparations to defend the passage of that river: they, however, quitted their ground on the advance of the allies on the 9th of that month, on which day the FOURTH HORSE forded the stream, and were afterwards encamped on the banks of the little river Lauter, forming part of the covering army during the siege of *Landau*, a strong town situated in the beautiful valley near the Queich. After the surrender of *Landau*, which terminated this splendid and memorable campaign, the regiment commenced its march back to Holland, while the infantry sailed down the Rhine in boats to Nimeguen.

1705

The winter was again passed amongst the Dutch villagers; and in April 1705 the FOURTH HORSE quitted their cantonments, and marching to the vicinity of Maestricht, erected their tents in the early part of May on the banks of the Maese, near Viset, where they were reviewed by the Duke of Marlborough on the 14th of that month. Leaving this place on the following day, they marched in the direction of Coblentz, and from thence through a wild and mountainous country to Treves, and were encamped beyond that city on the 26th of May. After crossing the Moselle and the Saar, on the 3rd of June they passed through the difficult defiles of Tavernen and Onsdorf, following the course of the Roman causeway over the heights, then emerging into the more open ground towards Tettingen, continued their route to the vicinity of Syrk, where they passed the night under arms; and on the following day encamped on the open grounds near Elft; at the same time the enemy occupied a strong position a few miles in advance. The Duke of Marlborough was desirous of carrying on the war in this direction, and the German Princes had agreed to co-operate with his grace; but their arrival was so long delayed that his designs were frustrated, and as the French were making rapid progress in the Netherlands, he was induced to quit his position and march to the assistance of the Dutch.

Accordingly, a little before midnight on the 17th of June, during a heavy rain, the army struck its tents, and the FOURTH HORSE, composing part of twenty squadrons destined to cover the movement, formed up to confront the enemy, while the army commenced the retreat, which was continued throughout the night without interruption from the French, and it re-crossed the Saar and the Moselle on the following day. On the 19th the retreat was resumed, and on the 25th the FOURTH HORSE and other cavalry arrived at Duren, in the duchy of Juliers. At the same time the French troops, near the Dutch frontiers, ceased acting on the offensive, and retired in a panic to Tongres.

After this long and difficult march, the FOURTH HORSE crossed the Maese near Viset, and were subsequently employed in covering the siege of *Huy*, which the enemy had retaken during the absence of the army up the Moselle.

The French army having taken refuge behind their fortificd lines, the Duke of Marlborough, after the surrender of *Huy*, resolved to attempt to surprise them in their formidable barrier, the construction of which had employed the space of three years. He accordingly, by a skilful manœuvre, succeeded in dividing their forces and in drawing them from the point selected for the attack. About eleven o'clock on the evening of the 17th of July the FOURTH HORSE, forming part of the division destined to force the lines, left their camp ground and continued their march throughout an extremely dark night, until about four the next morning, when the heads of columns approached the works at *Neer-Hespen* and *Helexim*. The guards were surprised and fled in a panic, the lines were forced and partly levelled, and the British horse were soon within the barriers; but before the regiments were formed, the Marquis d'Allegre appeared with fifty squadrons of cavalry and twenty battalions of infantry, and opened a cannonade from eight pieces of artillery. After the allied infantry had fired a few rounds, the Duke of Marlborough led forward the cavalry, which had passed the works, and the gallant British horsemen, by an impetuous charge, broke the enemy's ranks. The victorious squadrons afterwards sustained some loss from the fire of the enemy's infantry, but a second charge decided the combat; the hostile cavalry were routed and dispersed, several battalions of infantry were cut to pieces, many prisoners, standards, and colours were taken, and the FOURTH HORSE were once more triumphant over the legions of France and Spain.[31]

After this brilliant success the FOURTH HORSE were engaged in several manœuvres, and marches along the fruitful plains of the Netherlands; but the opposition which the British commander met with from the Dutch generals proved detrimental to the future operations of this campaign. In the autumn the regiment was with the covering army during the siege of *Sandvliet*, and after the surrender of this place, marched back to Holland, where it was joined by a remount of men and horses from England.[32]

1706

The FOURTH HORSE, with the other four English cavalry regiments on the continent, were now become a celebrated body of troops; and in April, 1706, when they again took the field, it is recorded that the officers and men looked forward with joyful anticipations to the events of another campaign. After traversing the province of Limburg, they joined the army at Bilsen, in the bishopric of Liege, on the 20th of May, and immediately afterwards advanced against the enemy.

On the morning of the 23rd of May the army was proceeding towards the Mehaine, and as the advance-guard, of which a detachment of the FOURTH HORSE formed a part, arrived at the uplands near Mierdorp, the enemy were seen traversing the plain near Mont St. André, their right stretching beyond the village of *Ramilies* towards the Mehaine; and their magnificent army, composed of French, Spaniards, and Bavarians, commanded by the Elector of Bavaria and Marshal Villeroy, was soon formed in order of battle. At the same time the allies made preparations for commencing the action, and the FOURTH HORSE took their station in the right wing of the army. About half-past one the battle commenced; but the British horsemen were kept in reserve until a decisive moment should arrive, when their well-known spirit and physical power would, it was expected, produce important results. The battle had lasted nearly three hours, when the Duke of Marlborough seized a critical moment to strike a decisive blow, and the British cavalry was brought forward. The *Fourth* and Seventh Horse, commanded by Major-General Wood, passed the little river Geete, and dashed along the plain on the right of the village of *Ramilies*, overthrowing all opposition, until they arrived at the rising ground behind the village of Offuz. The enemy was now in full retreat, and the two regiments went sweeping along the plain in pursuit until they arrived at the farm of Chantrain, where they overtook the Spanish and Bavarian Horse Guards, who, with the Elector and Marshal Villeroy at their head, were endeavouring to cover the retreat of their artillery. Having gained the enemy's left flank, the foaming squadrons of the FOURTH HORSE rushed upon the Spaniards and Bavarians, and, with one tremendous shock, broke their ranks in pieces! Then commenced the clash of swords, with all the uproar, strife, and turmoil of a close combat, while the Spaniards and Bavarians fell in numbers before the superior prowess of the victors; and the FOURTH HORSE took many prisoners, with the STANDARD[33] AND KETTLE-DRUMS OF BAVARIAN GUARDS, and the Elector and Marshal Villeroy narrowly escaped.[34]

After this noble exploit the FOURTH HORSE, having detached a party to the rear with the prisoners and cannon, continued the pursuit throughout the night until two o'clock of the following morning, making additional captures of men, artillery, and ammunition waggons, until the troopers and their horses were exhausted with the extraordinary exertions and fatigues they had undergone. Thus was one of the best-appointed and most gallant armies which France ever brought into the field nearly destroyed, and the reputation of the British troops and their distinguished leader exalted; while the result of the victory was the deliverance from the power of the enemy of an extent of territory exceeding the most sanguine expectation.

After a few days' repose the FOURTH HORSE were detached with other troops to summon several towns and fortresses in the Spanish Netherlands;[39] many places surrendered immediately, and renounced their allegiance to the Duke of Anjou; other towns, overawed by French garrisons, stood short sieges, but were captured before the end of the campaign, when the regiment went into quarters.

1707

Early in the spring of 1707 the losses of the FOURTH HORSE during the preceding campaign were replaced by a remount of 60 men and 94 horses from England;[35] at the same time the regiment was again supplied with ARMOUR,[36] and when it took the field it once more appeared as a corps of CUIRASSIERS. In the early part of the campaign it was encamped on the banks of the little river Sienne, and subsequently near Meldert. It was employed in several manœuvres designed to bring on a general engagement, which the French cautiously avoided. They ventured, for a short time, to encamp in front of the fortified lines which had served for a defence to their frontiers during the preceding war; but they made a precipitate retreat upon the advance of the allies, who continued in the field until the autumn, when they separated into quarters.

1708

The winter having been passed by the FOURTH HORSE amongst the hardy Belgians, they left Flanders in

May, 1708, and proceeding to the vicinity of Brussels were formed in brigade with the Duke of Schomberg's regiment (now Seventh Dragoon Guards), commanded by Brigadier-General Sybourg. They were afterwards engaged in several operations in Brabant and Hainault; while the enemy, taking advantage of the absence of the troops from Ghent and Bruges, obtained possession, by treachery, of these two towns, which had been the winter quarters of the English forces.

A series of movements at length brought on the battle of *Oudenarde*, which was fought on the 11th of July in the inclosures near the banks of the Scheldt.

During the early part of the action the five[37] regiments of BRITISH CUIRASSIERS, having crossed the Scheldt by the bridge of boats, were stationed in reserve on the plain of Huerne, behind the right wing of the army, ready to charge when the moment for a decisive attack of the horse should arrive. Advancing from this post they supported the infantry engaged, manœuvring so as to sustain the line in front, and to be ever ready to execute a charge, while their presence held in check several French corps; but owing to the local peculiarities of the ground, which was intersected by hedges, ditches, and rivulets, darkness put an end to the conflict before these warlike horsemen, who panted for an opportunity once more to distinguish themselves, were called upon to engage in close combat. The French retreated in confusion during the night, and at daybreak the FOURTH HORSE, with several other corps, were detached in pursuit; some slight skirmishing occurred, and the French took refuge under the cannon of Ghent.

In the movements which followed this victory the FOURTH HORSE took part, and they were subsequently employed in protecting the battering cannon, with an immense convoy of military stores, which were sent from Brussels to the army. They also formed part of the covering army during the siege of *Lisle*, an important and formidable fortress, protected by a Marshal of France, Boufflers, with a garrison of 15,000 men, and everything requisite for a successful defence; at the same time Louis XIV. commanded an immense army to be assembled for the purpose of raising the siege. But the allies, unmoved by the menacing manœuvres and threatened attacks of the enemy, prosecuted their purpose with vigour, and the vaunts of the French commanders evaporated in a short cannonade which produced little result.

The supplies of ammunition and provision for the besieging army having to be conveyed a considerable distance by land, the FOURTH HORSE were occasionally detached from the army to guard the waggons and cover their advance. In September an immense convoy, with ammunition and other necessaries, was despatched from Ostend under the charge of a guard commanded by Major-General Webb; at the same time the Count de La Motte advanced with 22,000 French troops to intercept this supply, on the safe arrival of which the fate of *Lisle* depended; and the FOURTH HORSE, with several other corps, were detached from the camp at Lannoy under Major-General Cadogan to the aid of the convoy. As the British squadrons approached the woods of *Wynendale*, a loud cannonade was heard; they instantly dashed forward, and the moment they arrived at the scene of conflict the French relinquished the attack, and the stores were conveyed in safety to the camp.[38]

After the surrender of *Lisle*, the FOURTH HORSE marched to East Flanders, and were engaged in military operations until *Ghent* and *Bruges* were re-captured, when the regiment went into quarters; and the losses of the preceding campaign were replaced by a remount of ninety-seven men and seventy-one horses.[39]

1709

After remaining in quarters in Flanders until June, 1709, the FOURTH HORSE advanced up the country and erected their tents on the plain of Lisle, near the banks of the Deule, where a vast and magnificent army, composed of the troops of several nations, extended its encampment in regular order over a large tract of country, and exhibited a fine spectacle of war. From this camp the FOURTH HORSE proceeded to the banks of the Scheldt, and formed part of the covering army during the siege of the boasted impregnable fortress of *Tournay*, which surrendered in the beginning of September.

From the banks of the Scheldt the FOURTH HORSE moved with the army in the direction of *Mons*, the capital of the province of Hainault, with the design of wresting this important place from the power of France. But while the allies were on the march, the French army moved from its former post and took up a position near *Malplaquet*, at the same time increasing the natural strength of the post by entrenchments and other works. In this camp were collected the choicest troops of France, commanded by two celebrated Marshals, Villiers and Boufflers, and opposed to them the victorious Marlborough and Eugene headed the heroes of Blenheim and Ramilies, amongst whom were the celebrated British Horse under the chivalrous Lieut.-General Wood.

On the morning of the 11th of September (N. S.), after divine service had been performed at the head of the troops, the battle commenced with an animation and effect which indicated the ardour that prevailed in both armies. In the attack of the entrenchments, and in forcing the works, the cavalry could not take part, and for a time the services of the FOURTH HORSE were limited to supporting the attack on the left centre, where the enemy's position was eventually forced by the infantry. In the midst of the arduous struggle, and while the storm of war was raging with dreadful fury, the Duke of Marlborough led forward the five regiments of BRITISH CUIRASSIERS, commanded by Lieut.-General Wood, and the Prussian cavalry, against the renowned Gens d'armes of France, who were instantly routed and chased from the ground; but as the British and Prussian horsemen, who were somewhat broken by the charge, continued their victorious course and swept the field in triumph, they were met by a compact line of French cavalry, consisting of the Gardes-du-Corps, Light Horse, Musqueteers, and Horse Grenadiers of the royal household, led by Marshal Boufflers, and these distinguished troops succeeded in driving back the squadrons of the allies. The British horsemen were, however, only repulsed, not defeated: they soon rallied again, and, glowing with zeal to encounter so celebrated an enemy, they returned to the charge, when their valour and prowess prevailed; and the French squadrons being driven from the field, the remainder of their army retired immediately afterwards, leaving the allies victorious, but with the loss of many men killed and wounded, and the pursuit was not continued beyond the village of Quievrain.

Thus ended a day in which the FOURTH HORSE acquired new honours. They were subsequently with the covering army during the siege of *Mons*, and after its surrender marched to East Flanders for winter quarters.

1710

The FOURTH HORSE, having been completed by another remount from England,[40] marched out of their quarters in the beginning of April, 1710, and advanced to the banks of the Scheldt near Tournay, where the allied army, consisting of the troops of several nations, was assembled, and, according to the journals of that period, the BRITISH CUIRASSIERS made a noble appearance.

From this camp the FOURTH HORSE advanced at five o'clock in the afternoon of the 20th of April, and formed part of the column under Lieut.-General Cadogan, which, after marching all night, surprised the French guard at *Pont à Vendin*, and penetrated their fortified lines without opposition.

The siege of *Douay*, a strong town situate on the river Scarpe, was afterwards undertaken, and the FOURTH HORSE, forming part of the covering army, were engaged in several manœuvres and marches to counteract the operations of the enemy, who menaced the besieging force with an attack; but the superior tactics of the Duke of Marlborough and Prince Eugene, with the bravery of their troops, prevailed, and *Douay* was surrendered on the 27th of June. After repairing the works, the army advanced towards the enemy, who, to avoid an engagement, retired behind their new lines of defence, when the allies directed their victorious arms against *Bethune*, and the FOURTH HORSE had their post in the besieging force until the surrender of the place on the 29th of August. They were subsequently employed in covering the sieges of *Aire* and *St. Venant*, and after the termination of this successful campaign returned to Flanders, where they passed the winter in convenient quarters.

1711

Advancing from thence in April, 1711, they directed their march to the banks of the Scarpe, and were subsequently employed in several manœuvres before the French lines of defence until the enemy's troops were drawn to the left, when the Duke of Marlborough, by secretly assembling a body of troops at Douay, forced the lines at *Arleux* and invested *Bouchain*. The siege of this place was one of the most difficult enterprises undertaken during the war, and the FOURTH HORSE were fully employed in the multifarious services required, the lines extending for many miles, and the greatest care and vigilance being necessary. In September the place surrendered, and this regiment, after traversing the recently conquered territory, to its former winter station, went into cantonments.

1712

It again took the field with the army in the spring of 1712, and advancing to the frontiers, was prepared to enter France; when the Duke of Ormond, who now commanded the British troops on the continent, received orders to cease hostilities, as negotiations for a general peace had commenced. In the mean time the regiment had lost its Colonel, the distinguished and spirited cavalry officer Lieutenant-General Cornelius Wood, whose death was occasioned by the fall of his horse; and he was succeeded in the command of the regiment by Thomas Viscount Windsor, from the Tenth Horse, by commission, dated the 18th of May, 1712.[41]

1713
1714

The FOURTH HORSE marched with the British forces from the French territory, and were encamped a short time in the vicinity of Ghent. They subsequently went into quarters, and these distinguished horsemen, after remaining on the continent until the treaty of Utrecht had given peace to Europe, were embarked for England, landed at the Red House near London in the beginning of April 1714, and having returned their CUIRASSES into store, proceeded to Northampton, Daventry, and Wellingborough. In the meantime the establishment was reduced from 400 to 226 officers and soldiers.[42]

On the decease of Queen Anne, in August of the same year, the regiment marched into quarters near the metropolis, where it remained until the arrival of His Majesty King George I. from Hanover, and afterwards proceeded to Gloucester and Tewkesbury. In October a squadron marched to Margate, and the remainder of the regiment was posted in detachments of two officers and twenty men each, between that place and London, to attend the Princess of Wales on her arrival. Her Royal Highness with the Princesses Anne and Amelia landed at Margate on the evening of the 11th of October, when they were received by a guard of the regiment, and on the following day they were escorted to Dorchester, where they were met by the Prince of Wales and the Dukes of Somerset and Argyle and the Earl of Bridgewater, and were conducted to the metropolis by the FOURTH HORSE on the 13th of October.

1715
1716

The peaceful accession of His Majesty was followed by the most strenuous exertions of many of the partisans of the Pretender; and in 1715 they broke out into open rebellion under the Earl of Mar. The army was immediately augmented, and ten men per troop were added to the establishment of the FOURTH HORSE. Upon notice of a meditated rise at Bath, this regiment, with Sir Robert Rich's Dragoons, took possession of that city, where they seized a great quantity of arms. England was at this period in great danger from the prevalence of jacobite principles, and the animosity with which two powerful parties in the state were arrayed against each other gave occasion for much alarm; but the staunch fidelity of the army overawed the disaffected, and the gallant troops who had so recently conquered the foes of Britain abroad, preserved the nation from the machinations of its enemies at home. The army, though on a reduced establishment, was in excellent condition, and the cavalry in particular was considered the best mounted of any troops in Europe.[43]

1717

After the suppression of this rebellion the King of Sweden espoused the cause of the Pretender, and made preparations for a descent upon Britain; and the FOURTH HORSE, with several other corps, were placed under the command of Lieutenant-General Wills, and sent to the north. This regiment was quartered a short time at Newcastle-upon-Tyne, and the Colonelcy was given to Lieutenant-General George Wade, who had distinguished himself in the war in Spain, by commission dated the 19th of March, 1717.

The project of Sweden having been defeated by the exertions of the British fleet, the regiment returned to the south of England, and took the travelling escort-duty for the Royal Family: at the same time the establishment was reduced to twenty-five private men per troop.

1718
1719

In 1718 the FOURTH HORSE were quartered at Nottingham and Northampton; and in November 1719 they were stationed on the Essex road, to attend His Majesty from Harwich to London, on his return from Hanover.

1720
1722

In the following year they occupied dispersed cantonments in Oxfordshire; in 1721 they were quartered at Dorchester and Salisbury; and in the summer of 1722 encamped near Andover, and afterwards on Salisbury Plain, where they were reviewed, with three other regiments of cavalry and seven of infantry, by His Majesty and the Prince of Wales, on the 30th of August. The camp was broken up in the beginning of October, when this regiment marched to Warwick and Coventry.

1724
1725
1726

During the summer of 1724 the FOURTH HORSE occupied quarters near London, and again performed the travelling escort-duty. They also furnished a party in constant attendance on the Prince and Princess of Wales. In the following year they occupied quarters at Stamford, Huntingdon, and Peterborough; and in 1726 at Warwick and Coventry.

1727
1728

On the accession of King George II., in 1727, the regiment marched to the vicinity of London, was reviewed by His Majesty in September of the same year, and was afterwards in attendance on the court until May 1728, when it returned to its former quarters at Coventry and Warwick.

1731
1732
1733
1734
1737

In January 1731 it was again on the King's duty, and was reviewed by His Majesty on Hounslow Heath in May of the same year. The two succeeding years were passed in country quarters, and in May 1734 it resumed its attendance on the Court. On the 29th of June following His Majesty reviewed the corps of Life Guards, when this regiment had the honour of furnishing the royal escort required on the occasion. In November of the same year, having been relieved on the King's duty by the Royal Horse Guards, it marched to Nottingham and Derby, where it remained until April 1737, when it resumed its station at Coventry and Warwick.

1738

On the 5th of July, 1738, the FOURTH HORSE, and the Royal regiment of Horse Guards, were reviewed by His Majesty on Hounslow Heath, and their appearance and discipline were approved of by the King.

1740
1741

After the review the FOURTH HORSE marched into quarters in Staffordshire. During the summer of 1740 they were encamped near Newbury; and in 1741 formed part of a body of troops encamped on Lexdon Heath, near Colchester.[44]

1742
1743

Towards the close of the summer of 1742 a British army proceeded to Flanders, to make a diversion in favour of the Queen of Hungary, whose dominions were overrun by the armies of France and Bavaria; but the FOURTH HORSE remained in England, and in the beginning of May, 1743, they marched into quarters near the metropolis, and resumed their duties of attendance on the Court. On the 17th of the same month one squadron was sent in pursuit of a number of deserters from Lord Semphill's (42nd) Highland regiment, a corps formed in 1739 of independent companies of infantry, raised in the Highlands, for service in the mountain districts during the disaffection which prevailed for some years in the north of Scotland.

The Highland regiment was designed for foreign service. In pursuance of this object it marched to the south of England, and on the 14th of May was reviewed by General Wade on Finchley Common, when the novelty of the scene attracted thousands of spectators to view the unique costume of the corps, and its appearance and discipline were generally admired. After the review the Highlanders were ordered to Gravesend, to embark for Flanders, but, as many of the men had enlisted on the presumption that they would never be required to quit the kingdom, and a report being spread amongst them that they were designed for the West Indies, a country which, at this period, was considered as a charnel-house for Europeans, about 150 of them deserted with their arms, and proceeded in a body towards Scotland.

The squadron of the FOURTH HORSE sent in pursuit of the Highlanders overtook them in Northamptonshire; and on Sunday, the 22nd of May, surrounded them in Lady-wood, near Oundle, and shortly afterwards the horse were joined by a squadron of Churchill's Dragoons (now Tenth Hussars). The Highlanders were disposed to submit on condition of receiving a *free pardon*; at the same time they took possession of a strong post in the wood, and, being provided with ammunition, they declared their determination to resist to the last extremity, and be cut to pieces rather than submit on any other terms. Captain Ball, of the FOURTH HORSE, had an interview with them, and, after trying every remonstrance and persuasion in vain, he was obliged to leave them. He, however, gained over two of their number, who conducted him out of the wood, and, promising them both a free pardon, he induced one to return and endeavour to prevail upon the remainder to submit. Eventually the main body surrendered at discretion, and were conducted to the Tower of London, where three of their number were tried and shot, and the remainder were drafted to different colonies abroad. This event did not, however, prevent the embarkation of the Highland regiment for Flanders.

1744
1745

In the beginning of 1744 the FOURTH HORSE were ordered to send a draft of sixty men and horses to Flanders to be incorporated in the three regiments of horse on foreign service. At the same time several additional corps were sent to the continent, but this regiment remained in the south of England until September 1745, when it was ordered to Nottingham; and on the receipt of information of the arrival of Charles Edward, eldest son of the Pretender, in Scotland, it marched to Newcastle-upon-Tyne, where several corps were assembled under the command of Field-Marshal Wade. In the mean time the young Pretender was joined by several Highland clans, and, there being but few troops in Scotland to oppose his progress, he gained possession of Edinburgh, surprised and defeated several corps under Sir John Cope at Preston Pans, and afterwards penetrated into England. At the same time Field-Marshal Wade marched with the troops under his command, by Durham, Darlington, and Richmond, in order to cover Yorkshire, and the cavalry proceeded to Doncaster, where the FOURTH HORSE arrived on the 8th of December.

Information having been received of the advance of the Highlanders to Derby, and of their precipitate retreat from thence towards Scotland, an attempt was made to intercept them, but without success. The FOURTH HORSE were subsequently despatched, with some other corps, under Major-General Oglethorp, in pursuit, and, after marching a distance of 100 miles in three days, in most inclement weather, and along roads choked with ice and snow, the King's troops overtook and defeated the rear of the rebel army on the borders of Lancashire, and captured several prisoners; but the main body of the Highlanders escaped, and, having placed a garrison in Carlisle, continued their flight to Scotland. The FOURTH HORSE pursued the Highlanders to Carlisle, and were stationed near that city until its surrender on the 30th of December.

1746

In the beginning of 1746 the FOURTH HORSE marched to York, and, after the decisive overthrow of the rebel army at *Culloden*, the regiment furnished escorts to guard parties of prisoners to Lincoln, and other places, in which service it was partially engaged throughout the summer; and in September it was stationed at Bristol.

The suppression of this rebellion having been effected, His Majesty resolved, as a measure of economy, to reduce this and two other regiments from the pay and quality of HORSE to that of DRAGOONS. The establishment was accordingly changed on the 25th of December, 1746, and, the pay of the non-commissioned officers and private men being reduced by this alteration, every man received a gratuity of three pounds, with the option of his discharge; and the men who accepted their discharge received fourteen days' pay each, to defray the expense of their journey home. The regiment was now armed with long muskets and bayonets, also with swords and pistols, as before. A slight alteration was at the same time made in the uniform;—the officers were distinguished by gold lace and embroidery on their regimentals, and a crimson silk sash worn over the left shoulder; the quarter-masters by gold lace, and silk sashes round their waists; and the serjeants by narrow lace on the lappels, sleeves, and pockets, and a worsted sash round the waist. When this change had taken place His Majesty conferred on the regiment the title of THIRD DRAGOON GUARDS, by a warrant dated the 9th of January, 1747, of which the following is a copy:—

1747

'GEORGE R.

'WHEREAS We have thought fit to order OUR OWN REGIMENT OF HORSE, commanded by Our trusty and well-beloved General Sir Philip Honeywood; THE QUEEN'S ROYAL REGIMENT OF HORSE, commanded by our right trusty and right entirely beloved Cousin and Counsellor, Lieutenant-General John Duke of Montague; and OUR REGIMENT OF HORSE, commanded by Our right trusty and well-beloved Counsellor, Field-Marshal George Wade, to be respectively formed into regiments of Dragoons, and their establishment and pay, as DRAGOONS, to commence the 25th of December, 1746: And,

'WHEREAS it is become necessary, by the said Regiments being formed into Dragoons, that their former titles as

Regiments of Horse should be altered; We are hereby graciously pleased to declare OUR ROYAL WILL AND PLEASURE, that Our Regiment of Dragoons, now under the command of General Sir Philip Honeywood, shall bear the title of Our FIRST REGIMENT OF DRAGOON GUARDS; Our Regiment of Dragoons, now commanded by the Duke of Montague, the title of Our SECOND REGIMENT OF DRAGOON GUARDS; and Our Regiment of Dragoons, now commanded by Field-Marshal Wade, the title of Our THIRD REGIMENT OF DRAGOON GUARDS, and have rank and precedency of all other regiments of Dragoons in our service. Nevertheless,

'OUR FURTHER WILL AND PLEASURE is, that the said three Regiments of Dragoon Guards shall roll and do duty in Our army, or upon detachments, with Our other forces, as Dragoons, in the same manner as if the word GUARDS was not inserted in their respective titles.

'WHEREOF the Colonels above mentioned, and the Colonels of Our said Regiments for the time being, and all others whom it may or shall concern, are to take notice and govern themselves accordingly.

'Given at our Court at St. James's, this 9th day of January, 1746-7, in the twentieth year of our reign.

'By HIS MAJESTY'S COMMAND,

'H. FOX.'

The establishment of the regiment, with the rates of pay of each rank, is given in the following table, copied from the War-Office records.

THIRD REGIMENT OF DRAGOON GUARDS.

	Per Diem.		
STAFF OFFICERS.	£.	s.	*d.*
The Colonel, *as Colonel,*		1	
15s.; allowance for		9	6

	£	s.	d.
servants 4*s.* 6*d.*			
Lieut.-Colonel, *as Lieut.-Colonel*		9	
Major, *as Major*		5	
Chaplain		6	8
Surgeon		6	
Adjutant		5	
THE FIRST TROOP.			
Captain 8*s.*; 3 horses 3*s.*; in lieu of servants 4*s.* 6*d.*		15	6
Lieutenant 4*s.*; 2 horses 2*s.*; in lieu of servants 3*s.*		9	
Cornet 3*s.*; 2 horses 2*s.*; in lieu of servants 3*s.*		8	
Quartermaster, for himself and horse 4*s.*; in lieu of servants 1*s.* 6*d.*		5	6
3 Serjeants, each at 2*s.* 9*d.*		8	3
3 Corporals, each at 2*s.* 3*d.*		6	9
2 Drummers, each at 2*s.* 3*d.*		4	6
1 Hautboy		2	
59 Dragoons, at 1*s.* 9*d.* each for man and horse	5	3	3
Allowance to widows		2	
For clothing lost by deserters		2	6
For recruiting expenses		2	4
For agency		1	2
FIVE TROOPS MORE, of the same numbers	42	13	9
Total per Diem	£53	15	8

Total per Annum £19, 630	18	4

1748

The regiment, having thus been constituted the THIRD DRAGOON GUARDS, was disposed in quarters at Leicester and Coventry, where it passed that and the following summer, and in the autumn of 1748 marched to Durham and Newcastle.

After the decease of Field-Marshal Wade, in February, 1748, the Colonelcy was conferred on the Honourable Charles Howard.

1749
1750

In the succeeding year the regiment was stationed at York and Barnard Castle; and in 1750 at Loughborough, Norwich, and North Yarmouth.

1752
1753
1754

In the spring of 1752 the THIRD DRAGOON GUARDS furnished a relay of escorts to attend the King to Harwich, where His Majesty embarked for the continent, on a visit to his German dominions. During the remainder of that year, and in the two succeeding years, detachments of the regiment were employed on coast duty in Suffolk, Essex, and Devonshire. Owing to an increase of duty on several articles of foreign produce, smuggling had become prevalent to a great extent in England, and it was found necessary to have parties of dragoons constantly stationed in the maritime towns and villages to assist the officers of the revenue in preventing the introduction of contraband goods. At the same time a laxity of morals prevailed amongst the labouring classes; and, in the absence of an efficient police in the kingdom, parties of dragoons were employed to patrole the public roads for the prevention of highway robberies, which had become alarmingly frequent, and were often attended with acts of cruelty and even murder. From the ephemeral publications of the day it appears that organized gangs of robbers infested many parts of the kingdom at this period.

1755

In 1755 signs of an approaching war began to appear. The French committed several acts of violence against British settlements in America; retaliation was made by the English troops, and the French were driven from the possessions they had seized. The British Court was disposed to an amicable arrangement of the existing differences; but such difficulties were raised by France, that his Majesty deemed it prudent to augment the strength of the regular army, and an addition of 1 corporal and 15 men was made to the strength of each troop of the THIRD DRAGOON GUARDS: and subsequently a LIGHT TROOP, consisting of 3 officers, 1 quarter-master, 2 serjeants, 3 corporals, 2 drummers, and 60 private men, was added to the establishment.[45] The general utility of light dragoons had been manifest in continental warfare; a regiment of light horse raised by the Duke of Kingston in 1744 had been highly instrumental in the suppression of the rebellion in Scotland; and from the autumn of 1755 light cavalry have constituted a portion of the British land forces.

1756

The aggressions of France in America were followed by a declaration of war; when the King of France made preparations for a descent upon England, which produced considerable alarm in the kingdom; but the designs of the enemy were frustrated by the warlike preparations of the British Government. In this year (1756) the establishment of the THIRD DRAGOON GUARDS was 24 officers, 7 quarter-masters, and 427 non-commissioned officers and private men.

During the summer a detachment of the regiment was stationed at Kensington to assist the Life Guards in the performance of the travelling escort-duty for the royal family.

1757

In July, 1757, the regiment was encamped, with several other corps, on Salisbury Plain, under the command of Lieut.-General Hawley; and a brigade was there formed of the LIGHT TROOPS of several regiments, for instruction in the evolutions, and in services peculiar to light cavalry. In autumn the regiment marched to quarters at Colchester, Malden, and Witham.

1758

The augmentation made in the naval and military establishments of the kingdom enabled the British Government to act offensively, and in the spring of 1758 the LIGHT TROOP of the THIRD DRAGOON GUARDS was called upon to hold itself in readiness for actual warfare. In April it was ordered to encamp near Petersfield, where a brigade was formed of the light troops of nine regiments, under the command of Colonel Eliott, of the Horse Grenadier Guards. Towards the end of May the brigade embarked on board transports,—forming part of an expedition under Charles Duke of Marlborough, designed for a descent on the coast of France. On the 5th of June the Fleet arrived in Cancalle Bay, on the coast of Brittany, and, having silenced a battery on the shore, part of the troops were immediately landed; when a battalion of French infantry and two troops of cavalry, posted on the heights near that place, retired without making opposition. On the following day the brigade of light cavalry and the artillery were landed; and on the 7th the whole (excepting three battalions of infantry left to cover the coast) marched to the vicinity of *St. Maloes*, and during the night the light cavalry, with detachments from the infantry, set fire to the shipping and naval stores at St. Servan, destroyed a fleet of privateers, with a man-of-war of fifty guns, and another of thirty-six, and afterwards retired. The capture of St. Maloes had been designed; but the expedition was not provided with troops and heavy ordnance sufficient for so great an undertaking; consequently that design was laid aside, and on the 11th of June the light cavalry were re-embarked. A second descent being rendered impracticable by severe weather, the fleet returned to England, and the light cavalry landed and encamped near Portsmouth and subsequently on Southsea Common.

A second visit to the coast of France was however determined on; and after several experiments had been made with flat-bottomed boats to ascertain the practicability of landing troops in rough weather, the LIGHT TROOP of the THIRD DRAGOON GUARDS was again embarked, and the expedition sailed on the 1st of August, under the command of Lieut.-General Bligh. After seven days the fleet anchored near *Cherbourg*; the troops landed,—the town surrendered,—the fortifications and works of the place with the shipping in the harbour were destroyed, and the brass ordnance were brought away as trophies of their success. A second descent was afterwards made on the coast of Brittany; but no advantage resulted from this enterprise; and when the troops re-embarked, the rear-guard was attacked by a considerable body of the enemy, and about 1000 men, with many officers of distinction, were killed, drowned, or taken prisoners.

In the mean time His Majesty's German dominions had been the scene of conflict and disaster; and a body of Hanoverian, Hessian, and Brunswick troops, commanded by the Duke of Cumberland, had been subject to a capitulation, by which it was agreed that the Hessian and Brunswick forces should return to their homes, and the Hanoverians remain in a district assigned to them: at the same time the Electorate of Hanover was taken possession of by the enemy. The conditions of this capitulation were, however, violated by the French; the Hanoverians resumed their arms, and, with the Hessian and Brunswick troops, amounting to 30,000 men, all in British pay, re-assembled under the command of Prince Ferdinand Duke of Brunswick, and had the advantage in several actions with the enemy. In July a British force was ordered to proceed to Germany, under the command of Charles, Duke of Marlborough, and the THIRD DRAGOON GUARDS were ordered for this service.

Previous to embarking they were encamped on Blackheath, on a fine lawn in front of the residence of Sir George Page, where they were reviewed by His Majesty in presence of a vast concourse of spectators, and their fine appearance was universally admired; at the same time the most sanguine expectations were entertained of the future achievements of this distinguished corps on the field of battle.

On the 27th of July the regiment embarked at Gravesend, and arrived at Embden, in Germany, on the 1st of August. On the 3rd of that month the troops landed a few miles above the town, where they encamped until the morning of the 5th, when they commenced their march up the country, and joined the army commanded by Prince Ferdinand of Brunswick on the 17th. On the 20th the THIRD DRAGOON GUARDS were reviewed, with several other corps, by his Serene Highness, who expressed his admiration of their condition after the march. They were not, however, engaged in any affair of importance during the remainder of the campaign; and they passed the winter in quarters in the bishopric of Osnaburg.

1759

The allies commenced operations early in the spring of 1759, and, having gained considerable advantage over the enemy in the country of Hesse, afterwards attacked (13th of April) the French army commanded by the Duke of Broglio in its position at *Bergen*. In this action the THIRD DRAGOON GUARDS supported the attack of the infantry, and were subsequently brought forward to menace the enemy's front; but it was found impracticable to force the position, and during the following night the allies retired, nor were they enabled to make a stand against the superior numbers of the enemy for some time afterwards.

During this campaign the regiment was formed in brigade with the Scots Greys and Tenth Dragoons: and on the 17th of July it was encamped on Petershagen Heath, a few miles from *Minden*, and near the strong position occupied by the

French army under the Duke de Broglio and Marshal Contades.

On the 29th of July the allies advanced and took post at Hillé, and the THIRD DRAGOON GUARDS were encamped on the extreme right of the cavalry. Prince Ferdinand having, by several manœuvres, succeeded in drawing the French army from its strong post in front of *Minden*, a general engagement was fought on the 1st of August, when the valour of the British infantry decided the fortune of the day, and the enemy, after a sharp contest, sustained a decisive defeat, with the loss of forty-three pieces of cannon, ten pair of colours, and seven standards. At the commencement of the action the THIRD DRAGOON GUARDS were posted, with several other corps, under Lord George Sackville,[46] behind a thick wood on the right of the army, and, although these troops were not brought forward in time to share in the conflict and glories of the day, yet they afterwards highly distinguished themselves in the pursuit of the enemy a distance of about two hundred miles, in which great difficulties were overcome, and several French corps were nearly annihilated.

The THIRD DRAGOON GUARDS took part in the several manœuvres and skirmishes of this campaign, which were continued throughout the year. In November the regiment was posted on the banks of the river Lahn, and it subsequently occupied cantonments near Osnaburg.

1760

In the spring of 1760 the enemy brought into the field an army of 100,000 men, commanded by the Duke of Broglio, with a separate corps under the Count de St. Germain; and so far outnumbered the allies, that the latter were obliged to act on the defensive. The THIRD DRAGOON GUARDS left their cantonments in the early part of May, [64] arrived at Paderborn on the 12th, and on the 20th encamped on the heights near Fritzlar, where they were formed in brigade with the First and Second Dragoon Guards, under the command of Major-General Webb. The enemy, superior in numbers and situation, advanced against the allies, some skirmishing occurred, but Prince Ferdinand was ultimately obliged to retire. Leaving Fritzlar on the 24th of June, the allies proceeded in the direction of the Dymel, and on the 9th of July the main army took post on the heights of Brannau. On the same day the First and THIRD DRAGOON GUARDS were sent forward to Saxenhausen, to reinforce a separate body of troops commanded by the Hereditary Prince of Brunswick.

On the 10th of July the Hereditary Prince marched towards *Corbach*, and when he approached that place he discovered a body of French troops formed upon the heights near the town. Imagining it was only the advanced guard of the Count de St. Germain's corps, his Highness determined to endeavour to dislodge them. The attack was accordingly made, and the intrepidity and firmness of the troops were conspicuous; but the enemy proved more numerous than was anticipated, and, being reinforced with fresh troops, it was found impossible to drive them from the advantageous post which they occupied, and a retreat was ordered. This was, however, rendered of difficult execution by the pressure of the enemy's advanced corps. Some disorder occurred. Several German regiments of infantry and cavalry were thrown into confusion, and the enemy, following up this advantage with a large body of dragoons and a numerous artillery, threatened the entire destruction of this portion of the allied army. At this critical moment the First and THIRD DRAGOON GUARDS were brought forward to undertake a service of great magnitude,—no less than to confront a torrent of superior and increasing numbers, and to drive back the victorious legions that were pouring down upon the allies,—a service which would at once attest the intrinsic worth of these corps; and their conduct proved their genuine bravery, and showed that the same valour, for which the corps had often been distinguished as the FOURTH HORSE, also glowed in the bosoms of the THIRD DRAGOON GUARDS. The two regiments instantly confronted the foe, and conscious of their own power they dashed forward upon the foaming ranks of the enemy, and used their broad swords with dreadful execution. The torrent of battle was arrested. The pursuing squadrons were driven back, 'mangled with many a ghastly wound,' and the remainder of the army was enabled to make an undisturbed retreat.[47] After driving back the enemy's squadrons the THIRD DRAGOON GUARDS retired, and joined the main army, encamped at Saxenhausen, on the same evening.

The loss of the regiment on this proud occasion was thirty-five men and thirty-four horses; with one man and two horses wounded.[48]

In consequence of some movements of the enemy Prince Ferdinand proceeded with the main body of the army towards Cassel, and on the 27th of July the troops encamped near Kalle. At the same time the Chevalier de Muy, who had succeeded the Count de St. Germain, having crossed the river Dymel with 35,000 men, and taken post on the heights near *Warbourg*, with a view of cutting off the communication of the allies with Westphalia, Prince Ferdinand resolved to attack him in this post. The attack commenced on the morning of the 31st of July, and the brigade of Dragoon Guards had another opportunity, which it did not suffer to pass, of distinguishing itself. The action had been maintained for a short time, although only a part of the allied army had reached the scene of conflict, and the English cavalry were a distance of five miles in the rear, but they advanced at great speed, at the same time preserving such order and regularity as enabled them to charge successfully the instant they arrived on the ground; and after driving the enemy's cavalry out of the field, they attacked the French infantry and chased them from the heights with prodigious slaughter. The town of Warbourg was carried. The Dragoon Guards, led by the Marquis of Granby,[49] pressed forward in the pursuit, crossed the Dymel, and the THIRD DRAGOON GUARDS, after acquiring great honour in the fight and in the pursuit, encamped that night on the heights of Wilda.

The regiment only lost one man and five horses in this engagement, with eight men and three horses wounded.

Notwithstanding the signal bravery of the British troops, the enemy, by superior numbers, was enabled to gain possession of several important towns; and, on the advance of the main army under the Duke de Broglio, the Dragoon Guards left their advanced post at Wilda, repassed the Dymel, and joined the lines near Warbourg on the 3rd of August. During the remainder of the campaign many brilliant services were performed by the British troops and their allies. By secret and expeditious movements, by daring and rapid advances, and by sudden and unexpected attacks, the enemy was kept in constant alarm; and this warfare of detachments, in which the THIRD DRAGOON GUARDS took an active part, prevented the French from deriving that advantage from their superior numbers which had been anticipated. At the conclusion of the campaign the British troops went into quarters in the bishopric of Paderborn, where they suffered great hardship from a scarcity of forage and provision.

1761

The French having, by their superior numbers, gained possession of Hesse and the Lower Rhine, amassed immense magazines of provision and forage in convenient situations; and having secured the communications necessary for their subsistence, they possessed great advantages over the allies, whose numbers were daily diminishing in consequence of privations.

Prince Ferdinand, conscious of the difficulties of his situation, formed one of those daring schemes which he knew the innate ardour of his troops would execute. In the most severe season of the year, when military operations were least expected, he made a sudden, extensive, and vigorous attack upon the enemy's cantonments, threw the French into the utmost consternation, and drove a superior army before him for many miles. Having taken several strong towns, and captured many of the enemy's magazines, the allies returned to their former quarters, and the THIRD DRAGOON GUARDS went into cantonments in the villages near the banks of the Dymel.

On the advance of the French army in the middle of June, 1761, the allies, having assembled from their cantonments, marched in several columns to Gesecke, and subsequently took post with their left on the river Lippe, the left centre under the Marquis of Granby at *Kirch-Denkern*, and the right extending towards the village of Werle; at the same time the THIRD DRAGOON GUARDS were posted on the heights of Wambeln.

The combined French armies, commanded by Marshals Soubise and the Duke de Broglio, advanced against the allies; frequent skirmishes took place in the early part of July, and on the 15th of that month a furious attack was made upon the post occupied by the Marquis of Granby; but the enemy were repulsed and driven back to the woods, where the fire of the skirmishers was kept up throughout the night. The division of the allied army commanded by the Prince of Anhalt having been removed to support the Marquis of Granby, a body of British troops, under Lieutenant-General Conway, took possession of the ground vacated by the Prince, being an eminence, between Illingen and Hohenover; and here the brigade of Dragoon Guards, commanded by Major-General Douglas, was posted. On the following day the French drove in the skirmishers, and renewed the attack with additional forces, at the same time extending the sphere of their operations; and an attempt was made upon the post occupied by the brigade of Dragoon Guards. The assailants were, however, everywhere repulsed, and they were eventually driven back with the loss of above 5000 men, 9 pieces of cannon, and 6 colours. Unfortunately the nature of the ground prevented the cavalry from taking part in the engagement.

In August the THIRD DRAGOON GUARDS were engaged in a general attack upon the enemy's posts, near the Dymel; and afterwards crossed that river and advanced to the vicinity of Cassel. In the early part of November they were engaged in dislodging a French corps from its post near *Capelnhagen*. On the 6th and 7th of that month they skirmished with the enemy's advanced posts at *Eimbeck*, in the Electorate of

Hanover. On the same evening the Dragoon Guards, with several other corps, marched through a heavy snow, and the following morning arrived at *Foorwohle*, where they erected their tents; but just as the encampment was formed, an alarm was given by the out-posts of the advance of the enemy in force. The British horsemen instantly formed, attacked the enemy with their accustomed gallantry, and drove them back with loss. Prince Ferdinand was a spectator of this act of gallantry, and expressed great admiration of the spirited conduct of the officers and men.[50] This warfare by detached parties, which occasioned considerable loss in men and horses from fatigue and exposure to inclement weather, produced no decisive results; and in the beginning of November the THIRD DRAGOON GUARDS went into quarters in East Friesland.

1762

In the spring of 1762 the allies made an excursion into the country of Berg, where they raised contributions. On the 18th of June the main army encamped at Brakel, where the First and THIRD DRAGOON GUARDS formed a brigade under the command of Major-General the Earl of Pembroke. On the 20th of the same month the army advanced towards the Dymel; and the French, under Marshals d'Etrées and Soubise moved forward and encamped at *Groebenstien*; when a favourable opportunity presenting itself, Prince Ferdinand immediately made dispositions for attacking the enemy.

Moving from their camp at an early hour on the morning of the 24th of June the THIRD DRAGOON GUARDS, forming part of the centre column, crossed the Dymel between Libenau and Silen, and took part in surprising the enemy in their camp, and in driving them from their ground, with the loss of their camp equipage and many prisoners. At the same time a French corps, consisting of the grenadiers of France, the Royal Grenadiers, the Regiment of Aquitaine, and othcr troops, under the command of General Stainville, threw themselves into the woods near Wilhelmsthal, to cover the retreat of the army; when the THIRD DRAGOON GUARDS, with the main body of the allied army, surrounded the wood, and nearly every man of this French corps was either killed or taken prisoner, two battalions only escaping.

The THIRD DRAGOON GUARDS afterwards pursued the main body of the French army in the direction of Cassel, and at night encamped on the heights between Holtzhausen and Weimar.

In the middle of July the regiment took part in an attack on the enemy's posts on the *Fulda*; and was subsequently engaged in several military operations on that river, and also on the Eder. By a succession of combined operations the allies compelled the enemy to evacuate a considerable portion of territory, and the campaign ended with the taking of Cassel. The success of the British army was followed by a suspension of hostilities, which took place in November, and the troops went into quarters in the Bishopric of Munster.

1763

The THIRD DRAGOON GUARDS having received, in common with the whole army, the thanks of Parliament for their eminent and meritorious services during the war, commenced their march on the 27th of January, 1763, through Holland to Williamstadt, where they embarked for England: the numbers of the regiment on embarkation appear to have been 14 officers, 328 men, and 434 horses, with 32 officers' servants, and 33 women who had accompanied their husbands through these long and toilsome campaigns.[51]

After its arrival in England the regiment was stationed at Canterbury; and its establishment was reduced to 28 private men per troop. At the same time the LIGHT TROOP, which had not been on service with the remainder of the regiment, was relieved from the King's duty at Windsor by the 15th Light Dragoons, and disbanded. Eight men per troop of each of the old troops were, however, subsequently equipped as LIGHT DRAGOONS, a practice which appears to have been general in the heavy cavalry regiments.[52]

In consequence of a representation of the increase of smuggling, and of the inability of the officers of the revenue and civil authorities to resist, successfully, the organized gangs which infested the maritime towns and villages, the THIRD DRAGOON GUARDS were dispersed in detachments along the Kentish coast, the head-quarters being at Canterbury.

1764

In April, 1764, the regiment was ordered to call in its detachments and march into quarters near London; and on the 14th of May it was reviewed in Hyde Park, by His Majesty King George III., who was pleased to express his approbation of the uniform and compact appearance of the regiment, and of the manner in which the various evolutions were executed. After the review the regiment marched to Leicester, Northampton, and Kettering.

This year His Majesty commanded the recruiting and remounting of the several cavalry corps to be submitted to the consideration of a Board of General Officers; and in consequence of its report, orders were issued for the recruits received into the regiments of dragoon guards to be from five feet eight inches to five feet ten inches in height; and that the remount horses should not be under fifteen hands, nor above fifteen hands one inch: at the same time the several regiments were ordered to be remounted with *long-tailed* horses: jacked leather boots were also laid aside, and boots of a lighter description were adopted; and the men were ordered to wear epaulettes on the right shoulder instead of aiguillettes.

1765

The reputation which the regiment had acquired in the field, and its uniform good conduct on all occasions, attracted the attention of the King, and in 1765 his Majesty was pleased to confer upon it the title of THE PRINCE OF WALES' REGIMENT OF DRAGOON GUARDS, in honour of the heir apparent to the throne (afterwards King George IV.), who was then in the third year of his age: at the same time it obtained,—as a regimental badge,—a coronet, with a plume of three feathers, a rising sun, and a red dragon, with the motto 'ICH DIEN.' In the month of March of the same year, it proceeded to Scotland; and in September Major-General Lord Robert Manners was appointed its Colonel in succession to Sir Charles Howard, deceased.

1766

In the spring of 1766 the regiment returned to England, and was stationed at Manchester and its vicinity. In July the DRUMMERS were taken off the establishment, and TRUMPETERS were appointed in their place.

1767
1768

The regiment left Manchester in April 1767, and proceeded to Coventry, Warwick, and Birmingham. In March of the succeeding year, the several troops assembled at Coventry, from whence they proceeded to Newbury and Speenham-Land, and after having been reviewed by His Majesty on Bagshot Heath, marched to quarters at Dorchester, Sherbourn, and Blandford.

1769
1770
1772

In 1769 the THIRD DRAGOON GUARDS were on coast duty in Sussex, with their head-quarters at Lewes. After calling in the detachments, the regiment assembled at Chichester in 1770, from whence it proceeded to the vicinity of London, and had the honour of passing in review before His Majesty on Blackheath. In May it marched to Colchester, Chelmsford, and Ingatestone; and in the spring of 1772 proceeded to Scotland.

1773
1777

After remaining in Scotland twelve months, the THIRD DRAGOON GUARDS returned to England and occupied quarters in South Britain, until the spring of 1777, when they again proceeded to the north.

1778

The nation was at this period engaged in a war with its North American colonies, and the French monarch having agreed to assist the revolted provincials, the army was augmented, and during the time this regiment was in Scotland, an addition of one serjeant, one corporal, and fifteen private men was made to the establishment. It returned to England in April, and in May a squadron was in attendance on the King and Queen at Portsmouth, whither their Majesties proceeded to witness a naval review, &c. In August, a further addition of eight men, who were to be equipped as light dragoons, was made to its numbers. During the summer it was encamped on Salisbury Plain.

1779

In 1779 the men of the PRINCE OF WALES' DRAGOON GUARDS equipped as light dragoons, with the men of the 1st, 6th, and 11th Dragoons were formed into a regiment, which was numbered the 20th regiment of Light Dragoons; and from this period the heavy regiments ceased to have a portion of their men equipped as light cavalry.

During the summer the THIRD DRAGOON GUARDS with the 1st Royal Dragoons, and the 15th, 20th, and 21st Light Dragoons, were encamped on Lexdon Heath, near Colchester.

1780

During the summer of 1780 the regiment was stationed at Shrewsbury, and on the breaking out of the memorable riots in London, it was suddenly called upon to proceed thither. Severe measures being found absolutely necessary to preserve the metropolis from destruction, the suppression of these riots was a painful service to the troops, and the violence of the misguided people was so great, that about

300 rioters fell victims to their own folly, before order was restored.

The PRINCE OF WALES' DRAGOON GUARDS returned to their quarters at Shrewsbury in July, where they continued for some time.

1782

On the 7th of June, 1782, his Majesty conferred the Colonelcy on Lieut.-General Philip Honeywood from the 4th Regiment of Irish Horse (now 7th Dragoon Guards), in the place of Lord Robert Manners, deceased.

1783

After the British Government had recognised the independence of the United States of America, the strength of the army was reduced, and the establishment of the PRINCE OF WALES' DRAGOON GUARDS was decreased 154 men.

1785

The decease of General Honeywood having occurred in January, 1785, his Majesty appointed Major-General Richard Burton Philipson Colonel of the THIRD DRAGOON GUARDS.

1788
1789

The regiment continued in England until the spring of 1788, when it again proceeded to Scotland, and remained in that kingdom the usual period of one year. After its arrival in England, in 1789, the establishment was increased nine men per troop.

1792

In August, 1792, the Colonelcy of the PRINCE OF WALES' DRAGOON GUARDS, vacant by the decease of General Philipson, was conferred on Major-General Sir William Fawcett, K.B., then Adjutant-General of the Forces.

1793

A further augmentation was made in the establishment in the spring of 1793, with a view to its being employed in actual warfare against the revolutionary party in France, who had seized the reins of government in that country, and beheaded their sovereign.

A French army under General Dumourier, having attacked the frontiers of Holland, a British force was sent to the continent under the command of His Royal Highness the Duke of York, to co-operate with the Austrians, Prussians, and Dutch; and on the 25th of May, four troops of the PRINCE OF WALES' DRAGOON GUARDS embarked at Northfleet for this service. Having landed at Ostend, they advanced to the vicinity of Tournay, and formed part of a corps of reserve to the covering army during the siege of *Valenciennes*, which place surrendered to His Royal Highness the Duke of York on the 26th of July. The siege of *Dunkirk* was next undertaken, with the view of replacing that fortress under the dominion of England, and the THIRD DRAGOON GUARDS formed part of the force employed in covering the operation. The enemy having brought forward an immense body of troops, attacked the covering army with great fury; when some severe fighting occurred, during which the THIRD DRAGOON GUARDS, owing to the nature of the ground, had to dismount and act as infantry; and the covering army, being eventually driven from its ground by the superior numbers of the enemy, the Duke of York raised the siege. The British troops afterwards returning to the vicinity of Tournay, were engaged in several skirmishes with the enemy; and towards the end of the year the THIRD DRAGOON GUARDS proceeded to Ghent and Bruges for winter quarters.

1794

Early in 1794 the regiment was again in the field; and it was engaged in the general attack on the enemy's positions at *Vaux*, *Premont*, *Marets*,[78] and *Catillon*, on the 17th of April; and was subsequently encamped, with nearly the whole of the British army, on the heights of *Cateau*, to cover the siege of *Landrécies*, which was undertaken by the Austrians.

On the evening of the 25th of April a French corps of about 30,000 men, commanded by Lieut.-General Chapuy, marched out of Cambray, and on the following morning advanced against the British troops. At day-break the enemy formed line, and being concealed by a thick fog, took possession of a village in front of the British position. At length their movements being plainly seen, His Royal Highness detached the THIRD DRAGOON GUARDS and other cavalry of the right wing, to turn the enemy's left flank; and this movement having been executed, the British squadrons charged with their characteristic gallantry, overthrew the troops of the enemy, and pursued them to the gates of Cambray. In the midst of the conflict the THIRD DRAGOON GUARDS, ever emulous of glory, were seen carrying destruction and defeat through the enemy's ranks; and in their victorious career, the allies captured thirty-five pieces of cannon, with a number of prisoners, amongst whom was the French commander, Lieut.-General Chapuy, who surrendered his sword to Major Tiddieman, the commanding-officer of the THIRD DRAGOON GUARDS.

The regiment, however, purchased its laurels with the loss of Captain Pigot, Lieutenant Fellowes, 1 quarter-master, 1 serjeant, 36 private men, and 46 horses killed, besides a great number wounded. His Royal Highness the Duke of York expressed his admiration of its conduct,[53] and inserted the following paragraph in the General Orders issued on this occasion.

'The Austrian Regiment of Cuirassiers of Zetchwitz, the Blues, the 1st, 3rd, and 5th Dragoon Guards, the Royals, Archduke Ferdinand's Hussars, and the 16th Light Dragoons, who attacked and defeated the principal column of the enemy on the right, HAVE ALL ACQUIRED IMMORTAL HONOUR TO THEMSELVES.'

After the surrender of *Landrécies*, the THIRD DRAGOON GUARDS marched to the vicinity of *Tournay*, and on the 10th of May were engaged in repulsing the attack of the enemy, whose troops were forced across the Marque, with the loss of thirteen pieces of cannon. The regiment behaved on this occasion with its accustomed gallantry; and sustained a loss of 2 officers, 1 serjeant, and 14 private men, with 25 horses killed; and 2 officers, 2 serjeants, 6 men, and 2 horses wounded.

The allies subsequently sustained several severe losses in actions with the enemy, and the Austrians having resolved to abandon the Netherlands, the Duke of York, who had maintained his position in front of Tournay against all opposition, was obliged to make a corresponding movement. The THIRD DRAGOON GUARDS shared, in common with the other regiments, the hardships which this event occasioned. In the subsequent retreat through Holland, which was occasioned in a great measure by the defection of the Dutch people, the incessant fatigue, the inclemency of the season, and the difficulty experienced in procuring supplies, reduced the British troops to a most distressing state of ill health, and occasioned the death of hundreds of brave men. At length the Maese and the Waal were frozen; the French, with their cannon and all the *matériel* of their army, passed these rivers on the ice: some hard fighting occurred, but the British, in their reduced condition, were unable to oppose effectual resistance. The army retired in the midst of a rigorous winter, through a hostile country covered with ice and snow, without necessaries, and without accommodation: consequently numbers perished from want, and others were frozen to death; yet the survivors preserved a firm and undaunted countenance, and defeated the attacks of the pursuing army. 'Such was the fate of as brave a body of men as ever Great Britain sent into the field. Both men and officers behaved themselves throughout the whole of the campaigns of 1793 and 1794, with a spirit that distinguished them wherever they were employed, and that fully corresponded with that idea of British valour, so justly entertained by foreign nations. It was, however, in the last stages of this unsuccessful campaign that their courage appeared with the most lustre. The undesponding perseverance with which they met and surmounted every hardship and obstacle, arising from the various incidents of war, was the more remarkable, that they contended against an enemy in full possession of every advantage occurring from victory, and whom they could only expect to impress with a sense of their valour. Herein they certainly succeeded.'[54]

1795

Having arrived at Bremen, in Lower Saxony, the troops there obtained provision and rest. The infantry embarked for England in April, 1795; but the THIRD DRAGOON GUARDS, and several other cavalry regiments, remained in Germany until November, when they returned to England.

1799

In the summer of 1799 the regiment was encamped near Swinley, under the command of Lieut.-Colonel Payne, and was this year ordered to be mounted on nag-tailed horses.

1800

It was again encamped at Swinley in the summer of 1800, and was reviewed on the downs by his Majesty King George III., who was pleased to express to Lieut.-Colonel Payne, through Sir William Fawcett, the colonel of the regiment, his high approbation of the appearance of the officers and men, and of the superior description and high condition of the horses.

1803
1804

In 1803 it proceeded to Scotland, and was stationed at Piershill Barracks, near Edinburgh; from whence it marched, in February, 1804, to Portpatrick, and embarked for Ireland. After debarking at Donaghadee, it occupied quarters at Londonderry, Enniskillen, Dundalk, and Belturbet.

On the 2nd of April, 1804, His Majesty appointed Major-General Richard Vyse to the Colonelcy of the THIRD OR PRINCE OF WALES' OWN REGIMENT OF DRAGOON GUARDS, in succession to General Sir William Fawcett, K.B., deceased.

1805

In the summer the regiment marched to Dublin, from whence it subsequently proceeded to Limerick, Fermoy, Mallow, and Bandon, and returned to Dublin in December, 1805.

1808

Orders having been given for the THIRD DRAGOON GUARDS to join the intended expedition to the Continent, one-half of the regiment embarked from Dublin and sailed to Liverpool, but the expedition, having been countermanded, on the arrival of the remainder of the regiment, the whole proceeded to Exeter, where the head-quarters were stationed until June, 1808, when the regiment marched to Dorchester; and shortly afterwards to Chichester and Arundel.

The THIRD DRAGOON GUARDS were present at the review which took place at Brighton on the 12th of August, 1808, in honour of the birth-day of his Royal Highness the Prince of Wales. They afterwards occupied quarters at Brighton and Lewes, and in the autumn they were called upon to hold themselves in readiness to proceed on foreign service, to participate in the victories gained by the British forces in Portugal and Spain serving under that illustrious commander, now Arthur Duke of Wellington, whose splendid achievements are interwoven with the history of Europe.

The regiment embarked at Portsmouth on the 5th of December, but afterwards disembarked and returned to its former quarters, from whence it proceeded to Hastings and other places in that part of the country.

1809

In March, 1809, it again proceeded to Portsmouth, where eight troops, of eighty-eight horses each, embarked on the 3rd and 4th of April, under the command of Lieutenant-Colonel Sir Granby Calcraft, leaving two troops at Blatchington, where the dépôt was established under the command of Lieutenant-Colonel Watson.

The Fleet sailed on the 17th of April, and two days afterwards the Doris transport was run down by the Bonne Citoyenne, in the Bay of Biscay, and thirty troop horses and two officers' horses were lost.

Having landed at Lisbon on the 26th and 27th of April, the Third Dragoon Guards proceeded to Belem barracks, and were formed in brigade with the Fourth Dragoons, under the command of Brigadier-General Henry Fane. From Belem they proceeded on the 4th of May up the country, and on the 10th of that month occupied quarters at Golegon and Torres Novas. On the 22nd the head-quarters were at Thomar, and on the 11th of June they encamped on the picturesque grounds near the banks of the Tagus at Abrantes, where Lieutenant-General Sir Arthur Wellesley had recently arrived from a successful expedition on the Douro.

Towards the end of June the army advanced. The Third Dragoon Guards left Abrantes on the 28th of that month, and, having entered Spain, were encamped, on the 10th of July, at Plasencia.[84] Advancing from thence on the 18th of July, the army crossed the Tietar, and proceeding along the romantic valley of the Tagus, formed two columns on the 22nd, with the view of attacking the French posts at *Talavera de la Reyna.* A body of Spanish troops came up with the enemy's rear-guard near the village of Gamonal, when 2000 French dragoons obliged the Spanish general to display his whole line of 15,000 infantry and 3000 cavalry; nor did the French horsemen attempt to fall back until they perceived the scarlet uniforms of the British cavalry on their right, when they retired; and the Third Dragoon Guards took a conspicuous part in the pursuit. They afterwards crossed the Alberche to Cazalegas, and took post in front of the army to sustain the Spanish corps.

The advance of a French force, commanded by Joseph Buonaparte, being immediately followed by the defeat and precipitate retreat of the Spaniards in front, the British commander took up a position,—his right on *Talavera de la Reyna,* and his left on the steep hills which bounded the woody plain; when the THIRD DRAGOON GUARDS took their station in rear of the left.

The action commenced on the 27th of July, and was renewed on the following day. A great part of the Spanish army fled at the commencement of the battle; the English, however, maintained their ground, and many of the Spaniards were induced to return to their posts. The several attacks were made with the usual impetuosity of the French soldiers. The advancing columns were, however, met with a firmness and constancy which confounded the assailants, and in every instance the enemy was repulsed and driven back with loss. On the 28th the THIRD DRAGOON GUARDS and Fourth Dragoons, having moved into the plain to the left, advanced to charge a column of the enemy's infantry, but the attack was countermanded, and the two regiments, after supporting the charge of Major-General Anson's brigade, were ordered to resume their former position. On this occasion Captain Brice, of the regiment, was severely wounded by a cannon ball. At length the enemy, repulsed in every attack by the British infantry, and driven back with dreadful carnage, retired, leaving seventeen pieces of cannon in possession of the English. The gallant bearing of the THIRD DRAGOON GUARDS in this action procured them the royal permission to bear the word TALAVERA on their standards.

Little advantage resulted from this splendid display of valour, the enemy having so great a superiority of numbers that, at the time the action took place, a French army, commanded by Marshal Soult, was advancing upon the rear of the allies. Information having been received that this force had entered Plasencia, Sir Arthur Wellesley, leaving the greater part of the Spanish force at Talavera, proceeded on the 3rd of August with the British troops to meet the advancing enemy. The Spaniards, however, ascertained that a French force was advancing on Talavera, and they instantly retired, leaving the British sick and wounded to the mercy of the enemy. At the same time Sir Arthur Wellesley ascertained that the force in his front was far more numerous than he expected, and he found himself in a critical situation.

The allied army did not exceed 47,000 men, and the greater part of these were Spaniards: the British, owing to the neglect and apathy of the Spanish authorities, had been some time without a regular supply of provision, and the strength of the men was exhausted. In front was Marshal Soult, with 53,000 men, in the rear was a French army of about 40,000, on the right were impassable mountains, and on the left the river Tagus. Under these circumstances the British commander resolved not to attack the enemy, but to cross the bridge of Arzobispo, and take up a defensive line behind the river. The bridge was accordingly crossed on the 4th of August, and by two o'clock the army was in position on the opposite banks. From Arzobispo the army proceeded towards Deleytoza, the THIRD DRAGOON GUARDS covering the retreat, and on the evening of the 4th of August they joined the camp near Truxillo. On the 10th they were again in motion, and having arrived at Merida on the 20th they encamped on the banks of the Guadiana on the 26th of that month, where they remained nine weeks. Extraordinary fatigue, added to a want of food, had already reduced the British troops to a very weak and unhealthy state, and whilst in this condition they were attacked by a malignant fever, which proved fatal to great numbers both of officers and men. The THIRD DRAGOON GUARDS lost on this occasion one major, two captains, two lieutenants, and many non-commissioned officers and private men.

The regiment was removed from the camp on the 28th of October, to quarters in the town, and it subsequently retired into the valley of the Mondego.[87] During the winter the Spanish army was defeated, captured, or dispersed. The British remained in Portugal, and their commander was created Baron Douro and Viscount Wellington.

1810

Before the opening of the following campaign the French army in the Peninsula was considerably reinforced; fresh troops, flushed with their recent German victories, were crowding into Spain, to the amount of nearly 100,000 men; and in the spring of 1810 the enemy's force in the Peninsula exceeded 300,000 men. The British commander could no longer calculate upon offensive operations: he, however, resolved to attempt the preservation of Portugal, and made his admirable arrangements accordingly. The ground fixed upon for a final stand was near Lisbon; but the troops continued in advance of this position as long as possible. The THIRD DRAGOON GUARDS were in motion on the 18th of February, 1810, and they arrived at Coimbra on the 23rd; advancing from thence on the 29th of April, they reached Mongauldo and Viseu on the 3rd of May, where a remount of thirty-five men and thirty-three horses joined from England, under the command of Captain Watts.

On the 13th of May Brigadier-General the Honourable G. de Grey was appointed to the command of the brigade composed of the THIRD DRAGOON GUARDS and Fourth Dragoons.

The French army designed to act against Portugal advanced, under the command of Marshal Massena, Prince of Esling, who, meeting with no force capable of resisting his numerous legions, soon took Ciudad Rodrigo, and invested Almeida.[88] Lord Wellington, having resolved to retire, sent the cavalry forward to Freixedas, and, on the 28th of July, the THIRD DRAGOON GUARDS took post at Minncae, while the infantry retired behind the Mondego, except the fourth division, which remained at Guarda. The explosion of the magazine at Almeida having decided the fate of that place, and accelerated the advance of the enemy, Lord Wellington fixed his cavalry at Celerico, with posts of observation at Guarda and Trancoso. The enemy advancing in force, the THIRD DRAGOON GUARDS, and other corps, retired on the 15th of September, passed the Mondego, and on the 19th encamped on a plain in front of Montagao. In the mean time a remount of twenty-three men and forty-seven horses joined the regiment under Cornet Homewood. The retreat was continued, and on the 23rd of September the regiment arrived at Busaco, and encamped at Villa Nova, in rear of the main body of the army.

The French army was marching upon Lisbon, and Marshal Massena vaunted that he would drive the English into the sea, and the imperial eagles should triumph in the capital of Portugal, when suddenly the rocks of *Busaco* were seen bristling with bayonets and streaming with British colours. On the 27th of September the French attacked the heights: ascending, with wonderful alacrity the mountain sides, they stormed the position; but were repulsed and driven back with immense slaughter. The THIRD DRAGOON GUARDS were in reserve in the rear, the conflict being on the steep and rugged sides of rocks and mountains, where cavalry could not engage. The enemy having failed in the attack, endeavoured to turn the left flank of the position, when Lord Wellington immediately retired. The inhabitants in the vicinity were all required to quit their homes and proceed with their provisions and movable property in front of the army, and the population (all orders, sexes, and ages) retired like a cloud behind the lines of Torres Vedras, where a series of works, connected with ranges of rocks and mountains, formed something like a fortified citadel of vast extent, which covered Lisbon.

The first range of defence extended about twenty miles; the second, and principal range, was from six to ten miles in rear of the first, and it extended about twenty-nine miles; and, at a considerable distance in the rear of the second, was formed a third range of defences: one flank was protected by a flotilla of gun-boats on the Tagus, manned by British seamen; and the other flank by the sea.

Here Lord Wellington resolved to make a decisive stand. The French commander was astounded when he discovered this formidable barrier, against which his superior numbers could not prevail. After making several reconnoissances, and skirmishing with the advanced posts, he relinquished his design and commenced retiring upon Santarem, when the THIRD DRAGOON GUARDS advanced in pursuit, and succeeded in capturing several prisoners.

1811

After arriving at Santarem the enemy collected his means, called to his aid additional forces, and prepared to make a mighty effort. The British army was also augmented, and the defences increased. At length the French army was so reduced from sickness and other causes, that Marshal Massena was under the necessity of retreating, and having destroyed a great quantity of stores and artillery, which he could not remove, he retired on the night of the 5th of March, 1811. The allied army moved forward in pursuit, harassing and attacking the enemy's rear with varied success. The French were guilty of the most enormous acts of barbarity and cruelty upon the unfortunate Portuguese peasantry; and, when occasion offered, the latter retaliated, so that the line of march presented a mingled spectacle of horror, carnage, and devastation.[55]

On the 15th of March the THIRD DRAGOON GUARDS had arrived at Condeixa, from whence Captain E. R. Story, (now Lieut.-Colonel,) of the regiment, was ordered to reconnoitre with his troop, and ascertain if the enemy were in possession of Coimbra, and while performing this service he fell in with a party of French dragoons, and took six men and horses prisoners. Captain Story ascertained that the Portuguese were in possession of Coimbra and of the bridge, and that the enemy had retired up the left bank of the Mondego: the troop then returned to head-quarters. On the following day the THIRD DRAGOON GUARDS were despatched across the

Tagus towards Badajoz, which place had recently been taken by a division of the French army, commanded by Marshal Soult.[91] Continuing their route, they had an encounter with the enemy near Badajoz on the 25th of March. The French sustained considerable loss, but the THIRD DRAGOON GUARDS had only two men killed and one wounded. On the 1st of April they were at Villa Vicosa, and on the 7th they crossed the river Guadiana at Juramenha.

On the 16th of April the camp broke up from Santa Martha, on which day the THIRD DRAGOON GUARDS, after marching five leagues, came up with a corps of French cavalry near *Los Santos*, and, notwithstanding the disparity of numbers, immediately charged, defeated, and pursued them above two leagues, taking nearly 200 prisoners: in this gallant affair the regiment sustained but trifling loss.

On the 20th of the same month the regiment was again in motion, and took post at Villa Franca. In the mean time Badajoz had been invested by the allies, and Marshal Soult was advancing with a powerful army, to the relief of the place. Marshal Beresford, who commanded this portion of the allied army, resolved to take up a position at *Albuhera*; when the THIRD DRAGOON GUARDS proceeded by Almendralejo to Santa Martha, and were at their post in the army when the French attacked the allied forces on the morning of the 16th of May. In the early part of the action the enemy gained considerable advantage: a powerful effort was, however, made by the allies, and 'then was seen with what a strength and majesty the British soldier fights.'[56] The French, repulsed and driven back, relinquished the contest, leaving thousands of their hostile legions stretched along the plain. The allied army also sustained great loss, particularly the English infantry. The THIRD DRAGOON GUARDS, commanded by Lieutenant-Colonel Sir Granby Calcraft, contributed materially to the success of the day: they lost one lieutenant, thirteen men, and twenty-one horses; and His Majesty King William IV. was graciously pleased, on the 5th of May, 1837, to grant permission to the regiment to bear on its standards and appointments the word 'ALBUHERA,' in commemoration of the gallantry displayed in that battle.

On the 18th of May the enemy retired, followed by part of the army, and by the cavalry, under Major-General Lumley. On the 25th the THIRD DRAGOON GUARDS and Fourth Dragoons were formed up in front of *Usagre*, when three of the enemy's 'chosen regiments (the Fourth, Twentieth, and Twenty-sixth) dashed through the town and formed rapidly on the flank of the THIRD DRAGOON GUARDS and in front of the Fourth Dragoons, themselves presenting two fronts. A charge of the THIRD DRAGOON GUARDS was at this moment ordered on the right, and a simultaneous movement of the Fourth Dragoons on the left.'[57] Major Weston, who commanded the THIRD DRAGOON GUARDS on that day (Lieutenant-Colonel Sir Granby Calcraft having been left sick in the rear) led the regiment forward with admirable gallantry. The charge was irresistible. The French, notwithstanding their superiority of numbers, were overthrown, pursued,[93] many of them sabred, and one lieutenant-colonel, two majors, and several other officers, with ninety-six non-commissioned officers and men were made prisoners; a great number of horses were also captured, the French dragoons having dismounted to effect their escape across a ravine. In this brilliant affair the regiment only lost four men; and, on the 27th of May, it returned to Villa Franca, having been nearly without forage the two preceding days.

Badajoz was again invested by the allies; and the enemy collected another immense body of troops, and advanced to relieve the place; when the siege was raised and the troops were withdrawn across the Guadiana. The THIRD DRAGOON GUARDS marched from Villa Franca on the 13th of June, crossed the Guadiana on the 17th, and encamped on the small river Caya, near Campo Mayor. In July the establishment of that part of the regiment which was on foreign service was reduced to six troops, making a total of 495 rank and file; and the supernumerary officers and men of the two transferred troops were sent to England.

On the 21st of July the regiment proceeded to Evora, from whence it marched, on the 1st of August, crossed the Tagus at Villa Velha, and proceeded by Castello Branco to Fondao, and subsequently to Alverça. On the 4th of September it occupied Ansale and adjacents; on the 25th it advanced to Guinaldo, to support the piquets; and in the night the whole retired to Quadrasages. On the 2nd of October it went into quarters at Avelans de Bon; and on the 3rd of December occupied Momento and Cea.

1812

Lord Wellington having resolved to besiege *Ciudad Rodrigo*, the THIRD DRAGOON GUARDS were ordered to advance and cover the investing army. They accordingly marched from Cea and Momento, on the 1st of January, 1812, arrived at Santo Spirito on the 15th, and established posts on the river Yeltes. *Ciudad Rodrigo* was taken by storm on the 19th; and for this distinguished service the Spanish Government elevated the British commander to the rank of grandee of the first class, with the title of Duke of Ciudad Rodrigo.

The siege of *Badajoz* was next undertaken. On the 27th of January the THIRD DRAGOON GUARDS marched for Freiz and Leomil, near the Douro, and arrived there on the 7th of February. On the 18th they were again in motion, and proceeding by Mysando de Corvo, and Thomar, crossed the Tagus at Abrantes, and the Guadiana, near Olivenza, and arrived at Rebeira on the 19th of March. Seven days afterwards they were again on the march, forming part of a force under Lieutenant-General Sir Thomas Graham, destined to surprise a body of French troops at *Llecena*: when the enemy, after some resistance, retired to Azuaga, from whence they were driven on the 29th of March.

The regiment formed part of the army of observation under Lieutenant-General Sir Thomas Graham, and accompanied the movements of this force until after the capture of *Badajoz*, when Lord Wellington marched with the main body of the army towards Castile. The THIRD DRAGOON

Guards were stationed at Villa Franca and Rebeira, being formed in brigade with the First Royal Dragoons, under the orders of Major-General Slade, and were attached to a separate corps of the army, commanded by Lieutenant-General Sir Rowland Hill: subsequently the regiment advanced to Llera.

On the 11th of June the enemy's General, L'Allemand, advanced upon *Llera*, with the 17th and 29th regiments of French dragoons. Major-General Slade moved forward with the Third Dragoon Guards and Royal Dragoons, when the two regiments made a brilliant charge, and defeated and pursued the enemy nearly three leagues. On arriving within a short distance of *Maguilla* the two British regiments had an opportunity of making a second charge, which they executed in gallant style, and having broken the enemy's first line, slew a number of men, and took many others, with one of General L'Allemand's aides-de-camp, prisoners. At length the enemy brought forward a strong support; and the two regiments being eager in the pursuit, each vying with the other which should most distinguish itself, were attacked by the enemy, forced to relinquish a number of prisoners, and to retire upon Llera. Major-General Slade concluded his despatch with observing, 'Nothing could exceed the gallantry displayed by the officers and men on this occasion. Colonel Sir Granby Calcraft and Lieutenant-Colonel Clifton, commanding the two regiments, particularly distinguished themselves, as well as all the officers present. I beg particularly to report the conduct of Brigade-Major Radcliffe, to whom I feel particularly indebted for his assistance on this occasion.' The Third Dragoon Guards had thirteen men killed; and Lieutenant Homewood, [96] sixty-seven men, and eighty-five horses were taken by the enemy.

On the following day a detachment from the Third Dragoon Guards and Royal Dragoons, consisting of about twenty men of each regiment, commanded by Lieutenant Strenuitz (aide-de-camp to Sir William Erskine) formed an ambush to intercept a strong foraging party of the enemy's cavalry. The party of the Third Dragoon Guards was destined to commence the attack, and was placed, for that purpose, under the command of troop-serjeant-major M'Clelland (who had formerly distinguished himself); and the Royals formed the reserve. The detachment came in contact with the French at a village near *Belango*; the THIRD DRAGOON GUARDS charged with all the spirit and fire of Britons. The fury of the onset threw the enemy into confusion; they at once gave way and fled in all directions, leaving several officers and men, and a great number of horses, in the hands of the victors. The success of this gallant affair enabled the regiment to retrieve, by exchange with the enemy, the greatest part of the loss sustained on the preceding day.

The French having considerable reinforcements at hand, Sir Rowland Hill retired by Santa Martha to Albuhera, where the THIRD DRAGOON GUARDS were joined by a remount from England, consisting of two serjeants, forty-two private men, and sixty horses.

On the 1st of July the regiment had another opportunity of signalizing itself in conflict. A strong body of French cavalry having succeeded in driving in the Spanish out-posts, was threatening the safety of the British camp at Albuhera, which was covered by the THIRD DRAGOON GUARDS, when a picquet of about twenty men of the regiment, under the command of Captain E. R. Story, who perceived the extreme danger of the camp and the necessity of a check, stood the charge of the French squadrons; and having ultimately received a reinforcement of a squadron of the regiment, under Captain Watts, repulsed the attack, charged in turn, and finally compelled the enemy to retreat, recovering, at the same time, the prisoners which the French had taken in the first onset. On this occasion Lieutenant Ellis, one serjeant, one trumpeter, and two private men of the picquet, were killed; and Captain Watts, whose squadron reinforced the picquet, was wounded. This important and valuable service, performed at so critical a moment, occasioned an order for every man of the THIRD DRAGOON GUARDS to be supplied with an extra ration of rum; and the following brigade order was published on the same day.

'Major-General Slade is most happy in the opportunity which the Third Dragoon Guards have afforded him of thanking them for the gallantry and steadiness with which they repulsed an attack made by the enemy's cavalry this afternoon; particularly the picquet under the command of Captain E. R. Story, and the supporting squadron, commanded by Captain Watts. He requests those officers, with the officers and men under their command, will be pleased to accept his grateful acknowledgments.

'The Major-General particularly regrets the loss of Lieutenant Ellis, who nobly fell at the head of his men: he has also to lament Captain Watts being wounded, but he hopes not dangerously so, and that the regiment will not be deprived of his services long.'

The camp at Albuhera broke up on the following day, and the troops advanced upon the enemy, who retired upon Cordova. The THIRD DRAGOON GUARDS proceeded by Los Santos to Llerena; and occupied Fuente del Mastre on the 24th of July, on which day they were suddenly called upon to make a flank movement with the view of gaining the rear of two regiments of French dragoons and one of chasseurs, who had driven in the Portuguese picquet, and were advancing upon *Villa Franca*. The regiment passed through Los Santos, and, advancing at a quick pace, soon reached Hinojosa; but the French had made a precipitate retreat, and had quitted the town a short period before the Dragoon Guards arrived.

After the main army had gained a signal victory at *Salamanca* (for which Lord Wellington was advanced to the dignity of Marquis), the French hastily retired before the troops commanded by Lieutenant-General Hill, who took up a position on the Tagus. The THIRD DRAGOON GUARDS marched by Usagre, Balangur, and Villa, crossed the Tagus at Almaraz on the 19th of September, and occupied Belois: from whence they moved on the 26th, re-crossed the

Tagus at Talavera de la Reyna, and arrived at Tombleque, in La Mancha, on the 8th of October; and, on the 21st, occupied some villages on the right bank of the Tagus.

The French army opposed to the Marquis of Wellington having been considerably reinforced,[99] his lordship retired from Burgos, and Sir Rowland Hill collected the troops under his command on the Jacamah, from whence he retired upon Anvalo. Having crossed the Manzanarus by the bridge Ponto Largo, near Arranheuse, the army took up a position, on the 27th of October, on the right bank of the river; and the light brigade of infantry was employed during the afternoon in defending the bridge, which had been mined for destruction, but the attempt did not succeed. During the night the THIRD DRAGOON GUARDS relieved the infantry at the bridge, two-thirds of the regiment having been dismounted for that purpose.

The troops retreating by Madrid, through the Guadarama pass, formed a junction with the army commanded by the Marquis of Wellington at Salamanca, the THIRD DRAGOON GUARDS, on this occasion, forming part of the rear-guard. During the retreat the regiment was joined by a remount from England, consisting of four lieutenants, two serjeants, two corporals, twenty private men, and forty-six horses.

On the 15th of November the army retired on Ciudad Rodrigo, when the THIRD DRAGOON GUARDS were again employed in covering the retreat, and suffered much from the inclemency of the weather, but more especially from the scarcity of forage and provisions. On the 20th they went into quarters at Herquera, and on the 27th proceeded to Membrio, where a remount, consisting of one lieutenant, one cornet, two serjeants, fifty-seven private men, and fifty-horses, joined on the 29th of November.

In a warrant, dated the 12th of August, 1812,[100] the facing of the regiment was changed from *white* to *blue*; cocked hats were replaced by brass helmets; jacked boots and breeches by cloth overalls and short boots; and the skirts of the coats were shortened.

1813

On the 25th of January, 1813, the six troops on foreign service marched to St. Vincent, where the forage being good and plentiful, the horses soon recovered their condition. On the 5th of March they re-crossed the Tagus at Alcantara, and on the 11th went into quarters at Gigo de Coria, where a draught of ninety-four horses joined from the Fourth Dragoon Guards.

Arrangements having been made for the advance of the army against the enemy, the THIRD DRAGOON GUARDS left Gigo de Coria on the 16th of May, and accompanying the second division, under Sir Rowland Hill, advanced through the mountains by the pass of Banos, and crossed the river Tormes below *Salamanca*. On the 26th of May they came up with the rear-guard of the enemy, covering the retreat from *Salamanca*, and being supported by the Royal Dragoons, and a troop of horse artillery, succeeded in taking upwards of 500 prisoners.

The enemy continuing to retreat, the allied army directed its march on Valladolid. The THIRD DRAGOON GUARDS crossed the Douro at Toro on the 3rd of June, and continued to press upon the rear of the French army in its retreat.

On the 21st of June the regiment, commanded by Lieutenant-Colonel Holmes, marched early in the morning towards *Vittoria*, where the French army, commanded by Joseph Bonaparte and Marshal Jourdan, was concentrated and formed in position. A general engagement immediately commenced. During the early part of the day the THIRD DRAGOON GUARDS manœuvred in conjunction with, and supported the attacks of, the infantry; but towards the evening they moved forward and made a brilliant and decisive charge on a corps of French cavalry and a column of infantry, which were covering the retreat of several pieces of cannon and a number of waggons laden with ammunition and treasure: the enemy was defeated, driven from his ground, and the guns and waggons were captured by the regiment. This was followed by the entire overthrow and defeat of the French army, with the loss of its cannon, ammunition, and baggage. The THIRD DRAGOON GUARDS had four men and six horses killed; Lieutenant Stewart was wounded in the body by a musket ball, but subsequently recovered; two men of the regiment were also wounded. Lieutenant-Colonel Holmes received a gold medal for his distinguished conduct in this action; and His Royal Highness the Prince Regent commanded the word 'VITTORIA' to be placed on the standards of the regiment.

The THIRD DRAGOON GUARDS were next engaged in the blockade of Pampeluna; and they were formed up in reserve at the foot of the mountains during the severe contest in the *Pyrenees*, on the 29th and 30th of July, but the scene of action was too mountainous for cavalry to engage.

The regiment remained in front of Pampeluna until the 17th of September, when it moved to Milagro, on the Ebro, where a remount, consisting of three officers, two serjeants, twenty-four private men, and fifty-five horses, joined from England, under the command of Major Watts. On the 20th of November the regiment occupied Valtierra and Arquedas, on the Ebro, where it remained in reserve during the winter.

1814

The movements of the allies were now attended with success in every quarter, and part of the army had already entered France. Early in the spring of 1814 the THIRD DRAGOON GUARDS advanced, by Pampeluna and Toloso, through the Pyrenean mountains, to St. Jean de Luz, in France, where they arrived on the 11th of March, and were there joined by a further remount of three officers, two serjeants, eleven private men, and fifty-four horses.

The regiment was now actively engaged in operations against the enemy, and on the 22nd of March had an affair with a body of French troops at *St. Guadens*, in which it captured many prisoners. Advancing up the country it was almost constantly confronting the enemy. The battle of *Toulouse* was fought on the 10th of April; but the brigade, of which this regiment formed a part, being attached to Sir

Rowland Hill's division, was not engaged. The enemy having retired from Toulouse, the THIRD DRAGOON GUARDS marched through that city, and on the 13th of April, being the regiment in advance, received the last shot of the enemy. The armies of the Continental Powers having penetrated France by the opposite frontier, had advanced to the capital, Napoleon Bonaparte was compelled to abdicate the throne of France, and the brilliant achievements of the British troops were crowned with the restoration of peace.

The THIRD DRAGOON GUARDS were quartered at Viellevigne; on the 25th of April they were at Nalloux and the neighbouring villages; and on the 25th of May occupied Venargne and adjacents. On the 2nd of June they commenced their march from the southern to the northern extremity of France, passing through many of the principal cities and towns, and finally arrived at Calais, where they embarked for England on the 20th of July, and landed at Dover and Ramsgate on the following day, after an absence of five years and three months. The loss which the regiment sustained from fatigue, privation, disease, and the various incidents of war, may be estimated by reference to the number of men and horses sent out from time to time to replace those which had fallen, or were become unfit for service.

On the 22nd of July the regiment assembled at Canterbury, and marched from thence to Huntingdon; where two troops were reduced, and the numbers of the remaining eight troops considerably decreased. On the 12th of August it marched for York, where it arrived on the 23rd, and occupied Leeds and Sheffield as out-stations.

1815

His Royal Highness the Prince Regent, appreciating the gallant and important services of the regiment, which, in connexion with the other corps of the army, and of the forces of the Allied Sovereigns, had been so conducive to the restoration of peace, was graciously pleased to direct that the word 'PENINSULA' should be borne as an honorary distinction on the standards of the THIRD, or PRINCE OF WALES' REGIMENT OF DRAGOON GUARDS, in commemoration of its services in Portugal, Spain, and France, under the command of Field-Marshal his Grace the Duke of Wellington. The Prince Regent's pleasure on this subject was communicated to the regiment by the Adjutant-General in a letter dated the 6th of April, 1815.

The return of Bonaparte to France, and the sudden breaking out of the war in 1815, occasioned an augmentation of two troops to be made to the establishment; and immediately after the battle of *Waterloo* the regiment received orders to proceed on foreign service.

From York it marched to Northampton, where it arrived on the 5th of July, and having established a dépôt of four troops at that place, under the command of Major Watts, the remaining six troops proceeded to Ramsgate and Dover, where they embarked on the 21st of July, under the command of Lieutenant-Colonel Holmes.

Having landed at Ostend on the 23rd and 24th (with the loss of one horse only on the passage), the regiment marched from thence to Drouges, near Ghent, where it arrived on the 25th. Advancing up the country it entered France, and proceeding to the vicinity of Paris, took part in several grand military spectacles and reviews, at which the sovereigns of Russia, Prussia, Austria, and France were present.

On the 29th of October the regiment marched to Fontenoy, occupying also Guitrancourt and St. Cyr; and while stationed there it transferred 108 horses to the 1st and 2nd Dragoon Guards, 3rd Dragoons, and 13th Light Dragoons; also exchanged 54 others. Leaving Fontenoy on the 17th of December, the regiment marched for Abbeville, where it arrived on the 28th of that month.

1816

After the definitive treaties between France and the allied powers were settled, the British troops withdrew from

France, excepting a small army of occupation. The THIRD DRAGOON GUARDS left Abbeville on the 15th of January, 1816, arrived at Calais on the 24th, where they immediately embarked, and landed at Dover and Ramsgate on the following day, from whence they proceeded to Romford, and a reduction of two troops was again made in the establishment. On the 12th of February the service troops marched for Leicester, where they arrived on the 19th, and joined the regimental dépôt. On the 23rd the regiment marched for Manchester, where the head-quarters arrived on the 29th, and detachments occupied Sheffield, Huddersfield, Leeds, and Liverpool. In May a draft of 184 horses was received from the Royal Artillery.

Towards the end of June the regiment embarked at Liverpool for Ireland, and having landed at Dublin, marched to Ballinarobe, Gort, Sligo, Castlebar, Roscommon, and Dunmore; and in August a further reduction was made in the establishment.

1817

In March, 1817, Lieutenant-Colonel Holmes received the ribbon and badge of a Companion of the most Honourable Military Order of the Bath, which was transmitted to him, in compliance with the commands of his Royal Highness the Prince Regent, by the Duke of York, in a letter bearing date the 11th of March, 1817.

1818
1819

In June, 1818, the regiment marched to Dublin, [106] Philipstown, and Tullamore. In the early part of the following year the several troops assembled at Dublin, and a further reduction was made in the establishment. During the summer the regiment marched to Cahir, Carrick-on-Suir, Clogheen, Fethard, and Newross.

1820

On the 25th December the facing was altered from *blue* to *yellow*, and the lace from *yellow* to *white*: but the officers were subsequently allowed to retain the gold lace as previously worn.

The regiment embarked at Donaghadee in August, 1820, landed at Portpatrick, and proceeded from thence to Hamilton, Glasgow, and Paisley.

1821

During the summer of 1821, it marched to Newcastle-upon-Tyne, Carlisle, and Penrith; but returned to Hamilton, Glasgow, and Paisley in August; when the establishment was reduced to six troops—total, 27 officers, 335 non-commissioned officers and privates, and 253 troop horses.

In November the regiment proceeded to Piershill barracks, Ayr, Greenock, and Perth.

1822

The whole assembled at Edinburgh in June, 1822, for the purpose of attending his Majesty King George IV., on his visit to Scotland; on the 18th of August had the honor of being present when his Majesty landed at Leith; and the King was graciously pleased to promote Captain Story (who was the senior captain in garrison) to the rank of Brevet-Major. His Majesty afterwards reviewed the regiment on the sands near Musselburgh, and expressed his approbation of its appearance and discipline.

In September of the same year the regiment returned to England, and was stationed at Newcastle-upon-Tyne and Carlisle; where it was frequently called upon to suppress tumults and disorders, and to protect the coal and shipping interests during the disturbances amongst the keelmen of the river; which service it performed to the entire satisfaction of Major-General Sir John Byng, who was in command of the district; and also of the civil authorities of the place.[58]

1823
1824

During the summer of 1823 the regiment marched to York and Leeds, and subsequently to Manchester, Nottingham, and Sheffield. In the spring of the following year three troops and head-quarters were removed to Liverpool, where they remained about a week, after which the head-quarters returned to Manchester. In April the silk-weavers at Macclesfield manifested a disposition to riot, but by the timely appearance of a detachment of the THIRD DRAGOON GUARDS tranquillity was restored.

In this year the regiment was supplied with helmets and bear-skin crests. In June it proceeded to Ireland, and having landed at Dublin, marched to Cahir, Limerick, and Clogheen.

1825

The Colonelcy of the THIRD DRAGOON GUARDS having become vacant by the decease of General Vyse, His Majesty conferred the appointment on General Sir William Payne, Baronet, who afterwards took the name of Galway, his commission bearing date the 2nd June, 1825.

1826

Towards the end of the same month the regiment marched to Dublin, where it remained until the following spring, when it returned to Cahir, Limerick, and Clogheen. Several changes of quarters were made during the summer, and eventually the troops were stationed at Cork and Fermoy, with detachments in aid of the civil authorities and officers of the revenue.

1827
1828

In the autumn of 1827 the regiment marched to Newbridge. In the early part of the following year four troops proceeded to Dublin, and subsequently to Dundalk and Belturbet. In April it embarked at Donaghadee, landed at Portpatrick, and marched to Piershill barracks and Glasgow, and subsequently occupied Perth, with detachments in aid of the officers of the revenue at Forfar and Cupar Angus.

1829
1830

During the summer of 1829 the regiment marched to Birmingham and Coventry. In October one troop was employed in assisting the civil power at Atherstone; and in the beginning of April, 1830, another troop was similarly employed at Pamswick. In the middle of April the regiment marched to Exeter, Trowbridge, Dursley, and Wotton-under-Edge. Towards the end of the year several changes of quarters took place, and detachments were furnished in aid of the civil authorities during the election of Members of Parliament. Eventually the regiment was stationed at Dorchester and Blandford; and an addition of three horses was made to the establishment of each troop.

1831

On the 22nd of April, 1831, his Majesty conferred the Colonelcy of the THIRD DRAGOON GUARDS (vacant by the decease of General Sir William Payne) on Lieut.-General Sir Samuel Hawker, G.C.H.

In June one troop was actively employed in suppressing the violent proceedings of the pit and ironfoundry men at Merthyr-Tidvil and its vicinity. During the remainder of this year the regiment was almost constantly in motion to support the civil power, and to prevent the occurrence of serious breaches of the peace. The labouring classes, being strongly excited by designing men, frequently violated the laws, and burnt great quantities of agricultural property.

The subject of a reform in parliament had created considerable discussion and interest throughout the country, and the resistance of certain members to the extensive changes proposed in the representation and elective franchise had excited the indignation of the populace in various places, particularly at *Bristol*, of which city one of the members, Sir Charles Wetherall, was recorder. He arrived at Bristol on Saturday the 29th of October, to open the King's commission, when he was assailed by an outrageous rabble, with insult, menace, and showers of stones. The tumult increasing, the Riot Act was read, when the mob became more violent than before,—broke open the

Mansion-house, demolished the windows, doors, and furniture, and prepared to set the building on fire. At this moment a troop of the 14th Light Dragoons arrived, and the Mansion-house was saved, and the rioters dispersed. On Sunday the mob again assembled, and plundered the Mansion-house, where they found a quantity of wine and spirits, and they soon became intoxicated. In this state the rioters became more furious than before. They broke open the Bridewell, liberated the prisoners, and set fire to the building. The new gaol and the Gloucester county prison were treated in like manner. The Bishop's palace, the Mansion-house, the Excise-office, the Custom-house, and many private dwellings, were plundered and set on fire, and several of the drunken rioters perished in the flames. In the midst of this scene of tumult and conflagration a detachment of the THIRD DRAGOON GUARDS was seen endeavouring to arrest the progress of the mobs. Unfortunately the magistrates did not give the necessary instructions; and as the soldiers were proceeding in one direction, destruction was going on in another, and property to an immense amount was destroyed, before the exertions of the civil and military powers restored order. About one hundred of the rioters were killed or wounded before the tumult was suppressed; and one hundred and eighty were committed to prison, of whom fifty were capitally charged with rioting and burning.

1832

In 1832 the regiment was stationed at Brighton, Chichester, and Worthing; and in August four troops proceeded to London, occupied Regent's Park barracks, and performed the duties of the metropolis during the absence of the Life Guards for the purpose of being reviewed by His Majesty. After performing this duty, the four troops returned to Brighton and Chichester.

In the early part of November, King William IV. and Queen Adelaide arrived at Brighton, and on the 30th of that month the officers of the regiment had the honour of dining with their Majesties at the Royal Pavilion: the band was in attendance during the evening, and also on several other occasions.

1833

The regiment received orders to march to Dorchester in January, 1833; and, before it quitted Brighton, Lieut.-Colonel Story was honoured with the King's most gracious commands—'To make known to the officers, non-commissioned officers, and privates, His Majesty's entire approbation of their conduct while at Brighton.'

1834

From Dorchester the regiment proceeded, in March of the same year, to Birmingham, where it remained the succeeding twelve months. In April, 1834, it marched to Liverpool, and, having embarked at that port for Ireland, landed in Dublin on the 1st of May.

1835
1836

After passing one year at Dublin, the regiment marched, in May, 1835, to Longford; remained at this station during the following twelve months, and proceeded, in May, 1836, to Ballincollig.

1837
1838

Having spent a period of three years in Ireland, the regiment marched to Cork; embarked from thence on the 14th of June, 1837, for England; landed at Bristol on the following day, and proceeded to Ipswich; where it has remained until the spring of 1838, which brings the record of this distinguished corps to a conclusion.

Few cavalry regiments have been favoured with a greater number of opportunities of acquiring honour by deeds of valour in action with the enemies of the British nation than the THIRD, OR PRINCE OF WALES' REGIMENT OF DRAGOON GUARDS: it has served under MARLBOROUGH and WELLINGTON—names immortalized in the history of Europe. As a regiment of HORSE, it fought at Blenheim, Ramilies, and Malplaquet—battles which shed lustre on the British arms. As a corps of DRAGOON GUARDS, it gained immortal fame at Corbach and Warbourg, and signalized itself in other actions in Germany. In Flanders, under his Royal Highness the Duke of York, it earned new laurels; and, in the Peninsular War, it added to its previous reputation by its gallant bearing on all occasions, particularly at the battle of Albuhera. On this subject, Viscount Beresford observed, in a letter to the Adjutant-General, 'The conduct of this regiment, during the period it was under my command, deserved, on all occasions, and especially at the battle of Albuhera, my highest encomiums.' On home service, it has acquired the confidence and approbation of its sovereign, and the commendations of the general officers under whose command it has been placed.

Third Dragoon Guards, 1838. [To face page 112.

FOOTNOTES:

[7]See a brief memoir of this nobleman in the succession of Colonels at page 113.

[8]'JAMES, R.

'THESE ARE TO AUTHORIZE YOU to raise volunteers with able horses for one troop of Horse, which you are commissioned to raise and command for Our Service, consisting of threescore soldiers, three corporals, and two trumpeters, besides Commissioned Officers. And as you shall raise the said Volunteers and Non-commissioned Officers of Our said troop, you are to give notice thereof to our Commissary General when and where you shall have twenty soldiers ready, with their horses, together, besides officers; that he, or his deputy, may muster them accordingly, and from such muster those soldiers, with all the officers of the said troop, are to commence and be in our pay; and from thenceforth as you shall, from time to time, entertain any more soldiers with their horses fit for Our Service, and shall produce them to muster, they shall be respectively mustered thereupon, until you shall have threescore soldiers, besides officers; and when that number shall be fully, or nearly, completed, they are to be sent under the command of a Commissioned Officer to Worcester and Droytwich, (appointed for the quarters of Our said troop,) where they are also to be mustered, and soe remain until further orders. You are likewise to send a trusty person to Our Tower of London to receive arms for Our said troop.

'WHEREIN, all Magistrates, Justices of the Peace, and Constables, whom it may concern, are required to be assisting; and the Officers are to be careful that the soldiers behave themselves civilly, and duly pay their landlords.

'GIVEN at Our Court at Whitehall, this 23rd day of June, 1685, in the first year of Our Reign.

'BY HIS MAJESTY'S COMMAND,

'WILLIAM BLATHWAYTE.'

'To *Our right trusty and right well-beloved Cousin and Councillor, Thomas Earl of Plymouth, &c.*'

A similar warrant was issued for raising each of the other five troops.—*War-Office Records.*

[9]The cuirass was not peculiar to this regiment, there being, in the autumn of 1685, ten regiments of Cuirassiers in the English army, besides the Life Guards, who were also Cuirassiers.

[10]War-Office Records.

[11]The Marquis de Miremont was a French nobleman, and cousin to Louis Earl of Feversham.

[12]The three regiments were Colonel John Butler's Dragoons, Colonel Anthony Hamilton's Foot Guards, and Colonel Roger McElligot's Regiment of Foot—1500 men.—*War-Office Records.*

[13]Memoirs of General Mackay.

[14]Mackay's Memoirs, p. 56.

[15]London Gazette.

[16]War-Office Records.

[17]D'Auvergne's History of the Campaigns in Flanders, &c.

[18]No record appears to have been preserved of the number killed and wounded of the FOURTH HORSE; but according to the London Gazette, No. 2895, the English cavalry lost 59 officers and 472 men.

[19]D'Auvergne's History of the Campaigns in Flanders; Boyer's Life of King William III.; the London Gazette, &c.

[20]The present Second and Sixth Dragoon Guards:—Galway's Horse was disbanded after the Peace of Ryswick in 1697.

[21]D'Auvergne.

[22]'The Queen's Horse, now 1st Dragoon Guards; Carabiniers, now 6th Dragoon Guards; a squadron of Schomberg's Horse, now 7th Dragoon Guards; with Stewart's and Stanley's Foot.'—*London Gazette* and *Millner's Journal.*

[23]'On the 31st of October the garrison marched out of the place, being upwards of 1500 men, besides nearly 300

that deserted before the capitulation. The troops of Liege came out first, and immediately quitted the French service, marching off in a body. Of the Swiss there deserted likewise above 400 as soon as they came out; so that this garrison will be very much lessened before they get to Antwerp, whither they are marching, being conducted by a squadron of Brigadier-General Wood's regiment.'—*London Gazette, No. 3857.*

[24]'We generally began our march about three in the morning, proceeded about four leagues, or four and a half, each day, and reached our ground about nine. As we marched through the countries of our Allies, commissaries were appointed, to furnish us with all manner of necessaries for man and horse; these were brought to the ground before we arrived, and the soldiers had nothing to do but to pitch their tents, boil their kettles, and lie down to rest. Surely never was such a march carried on with more regularity, and with less fatigue both to man and horse.'—*Parker's Memoirs.*

[25]'All the troops in general behaved with the greatest bravery, but none distinguished themselves more than Her Majesty of Great Britain's subjects, who in this engagement had the post of honour, which they sustained with the universal applause and approbation of all the Generals of the several nations who were eye-witnesses of their courage and resolution.'—*London Gazette, No. 4033.*

[26]Annals of Queen Anne; Millner's Journal; Military History of Marlborough and Prince Eugene, &c. &c.

[27]Parker's Memoirs.

[28]'Here was a fine plain, without hedge or ditch, for the Cavalry on both sides to show their bravery; for there were but few Foot to interpose, these being mostly engaged at the villages.

'And now our squadrons charged in their turn, and thus for some hours they charged each other with various success, all sword in hand. At length the French courage began to abate, and our squadrons gained upon them.'—*Parker's Memoirs.*

[29]'The bravery of all our troops on this occasion cannot be expressed; the Generals, as well as the officers and soldiers, behaving themselves with the greatest courage and resolution, the Horse and Dragoons having been obliged to charge four or five several times.'—*The Duke of Marlborough's Despatch.*

[30]'Not only Fame, but likewise the Generals of my forces—the companions of your labours and victories—attributed the same chiefly to your counsels, and the valour and bravery of the *English*, and other forces who fought under your conduct.'—*The Emperor of Germany's Letter to the Duke of Marlborough.*

[31]'The troops acquitted themselves with a bravery surpassing all that could have been hoped of them.'—*Marlborough's Despatch.*

[32]War-Office Records.

[33]'The headmost regiments of English Horse that pursued the enemy's centre were those of Major-General Wood, commanded by himself, and Wyndham's Carabiniers, headed by Major Pertry. When they came upon a rising ground they espied seven squadrons of the Spanish and Bavarian Guards, with whom the Elector of Bavaria and Marshal Villeroy hoped to make good their retreat and save their cannon, which was marching in a line before them. General Wood gallopped with his own regiment upon the enemy's left, and charged them so vigorously that he broke them all to pieces, killing many of them and taking not a few prisoners, amongst whom were two Lieut.-Colonels, one Major, four Captains, with several subalterns and men. *He took also the Standard of the Elector's Guard*, two of the Elector's own Trumpeters, and killed his Kettle-Drummer, the Elector himself and Marshal Villeroy narrowly escaping.'—*Annals of Queen Anne.*

[34]'One of the Lieut.-Colonels, who was much wounded, remembering me last war, cried out to me to save his life, which I did. The other Lieut.-Colonel came to me and yielded himself prisoner also. Both these assured me the day after the battle, that the Elector himself and Marshal Villeroy were in the crowd, and not ten yards from me when they two called out to me for quarter, and that they narrowly escaped us; which, had I been so fortunate as to have known, I had strained Coriolanus (on whom I rid all the day of the battle) to have made them prisoners.'—*Extract of a Letter from Lieut.-General Wood.*

[35]War-Office Records.

[36]London Gazette.

[37]Now the First, Third, Fifth, Sixth, and Seventh Dragoon Guards.

[38]Major-General Webb received the thanks of Parliament for his excellent defence of the convoy.

[39]War Office Records.

[40]War Office Records.

[41]The Tenth Horse was raised in February, 1693, and disbanded after the peace of Utrecht.

[42]War-Office Records, London Gazette, &c. &c.

[43]Annals of George I., vol. iii., p. 179.

[44]The following corps were encamped on Lexdon Heath: Horse—Pembroke's, Montague's, and Wade's (First, Second, and Third Dragoon Guards); Dragoons—Hawley's, Campbell's, Honeywood's, and Cadogan's (First, Second, Third and Sixth); with seven regiments of Foot, viz., Third, Eleventh, Twelfth, Thirteenth, Twenty-first, Twenty-third, and Thirty-first.

[45]War-Office Establishment Book.

[46]List of cavalry corps of the right wing under Lord George Sackville, at the battle of Minden.

1st Brigade.—Blues, 1st Dragoon Guards, and Inniskilling Dragoons.

2nd Brigade.—3rd Dragoon Guards, Scots Greys, and 10th Dragoons.

Hanoverian Regiments of Bremen and Veltheim.—*History of the Campaign in Germany.*

[47]'Bland's squadrons and Howard's Regiment of Dragoons (First and Third Dragoon Guards) *charged* the enemy *so furiously* as to enable our infantry to make a safe retreat.'—*London Gazette.*

'The Hereditary Prince, as a last resource, put himself at the head of a squadron of Bland's and Howard's Regiment of Dragoons. By these the uncommon heroism of their young leader was perfectly seconded. *They charged the enemy with the utmost fury, stopped the career of their victorious horse, and enabled the allied battalions to make an undisturbed retreat.'—Annual Register, 1760.*

'Bland's squadrons and Howard's Regiment of Dragoons MADE A MOST FURIOUS CHARGE ON THE ENEMY.'—*Operations of the Allied Army. London, 1764.*

'One squadron of Bland's, commanded by Major Mill, and Howard's Regiment of Dragoons gained great honour.'—*Ibid.*

[48]London Gazette.

[49]'My Lord Granby, with the English cavalry, contributed materially to the success of the day.'—*Prince Ferdinand's Despatch.*

'I should do injustice to the general officers, and *to every officer and private man of the cavalry,* if I did not beg your Lordship would assure His Majesty that *nothing could exceed their gallant behaviour on that occasion.'—The Marquis of Granby's Despatch.*

'The English cavalry outdid his (Prince Ferdinand's) expectation, and indeed all former examples. They came up five miles on a full trot (the Germans call it a gallop) without being blown, without the least confusion or disorder, and attacked the enemy's cavalry and infantry several times.'—*Annual Register, 1760.*

[50]London Gazette.

[51]It appears from the Official Returns that no less than 1666 women were with the British army in Germany.

[52]Records in the Adjutant-General's Office.

[53]

Heights above Cateau, 26th April, 1794.

'SIR,

'It is from the field of battle that I have the satisfaction to acquaint you, for His Majesty's information, with the glorious success which the army under my command has had this day.

'At day-break this morning the enemy attacked me on all sides. After a short but severe conflict, we succeeded in repulsing them with considerable slaughter.

'The enemy's General Chapuy is taken prisoner, and we are masters of thirty-five pieces of the enemy's cannon. THE BEHAVIOUR OF THE BRITISH CAVALRY HAS BEEN BEYOND ALL PRAISE. It is impossible for me, as yet, to give a full account of the loss sustained by His Majesty's troops: I have reason to believe that it is not considerable. The only officers of whom I have any information as yet, and who I believe are all that have fallen upon this occasion, are Major-General Mansell, Captain Pigot, and Lieutenant Fellowes, of the THIRD DRAGOON GUARDS.'—*Extract from the Duke of York's Despatch.*

[54]Annual Register.

[55]'Every horror that could make war hideous attended this dreadful march! Distress, conflagration, death, in all modes! from wounds, from fatigue, from water, from the flames, from starvation. On every side unlimited violence—unlimited vengeance.'—*Napier.*

'This retreat has been marked by a barbarity seldom equalled and never surpassed.'—Lord Wellington's Despatch.

[56]Colonel Napier.

[57]Major-General Lumley's Despatch.

[58]

'Newcastle-upon-Tyne,
10th December, 1822.

'Sir,

'I have the honor to announce to you the happy termination of the disturbances amongst the keelmen of this river, and at the same time to express the gratitude of the civil authorities for the promptitude with which Colonel Holmes of the Third Dragoon Guards has afforded them support on all occasions, and their entire approbation of the conduct of the troops under his command.

'I have, &c.
'ROBERT BELL, Mayor.

'To Major-General Sir John Byng, K.C.B.'

SUCCESSION OF COLONELS

OF THE

THIRD, OR PRINCE OF WALES' REGIMENT

OF DRAGOON GUARDS.

THOMAS EARL OF PLYMOUTH,

Appointed 15th July, 1685.

On the decease of THOMAS, sixth LORD WINDSOR, on the 6th of December, 1642, without issue, his titles became extinct, but his estates descended to his nephew THOMAS WINDSOR HICKMAN, then in the fifteenth year of his age. The rebellion breaking out immediately, this youth displayed an ardent and chivalrous spirit, with a fixed devotion to his sovereign and to monarchical government. He raised and maintained a troop of horse at his own charge, with which he joined King Charles I., and became an active and an enterprising leader amongst the loyalists, distinguishing himself in many skirmishes and sharp encounters with the rebels. At the battle of *Naseby*, fought on the 14th of June, 1645, he commanded a regiment of horse, and stoutly charged through and through the enemy's ranks; when the King, taking special notice of the gallantry of this youth, commanded that that regiment, with its valiant leader, should be the royal guard for that day. The King's army was, however, defeated, and his Majesty retreated to Ashby-de-la-Zouch, in Leicestershire; where, remembering the signal service of that regiment of horse, and the particular merits of Colonel Windsor Hickman, he gave command for preparing a patent for reviving the title and dignity of LORD WINDSOR, to the said THOMAS WINDSOR HICKMAN.[114] But, from that period, a series of disasters befalling the unfortunate monarch, nothing further transpired on that subject until the restoration of King Charles II., when his Majesty, taking into consideration the many good services performed by this THOMAS WINDSOR HICKMAN throughout the whole course of that rebellion (amongst which the raising of the siege of his Majesty's garrison of High-Ercall, in Shropshire, was not the least), as also his sufferings in the Royal cause, by imprisonment, plunder, and otherwise, did, by a declaratory patent under the great seal, bearing date the 16th of June, 1660, restore unto him the title and dignity of LORD WINDSOR, with the same rank and precedence which were held by his maternal uncle, Thomas, late Lord Windsor.

On the 18th of July following, LORD WINDSOR was appointed lord-lieutenant of Worcestershire; and, in 1665, he was sent governor to Jamaica. During his stay in the West Indies, LORD WINDSOR assembled the troops under his command, defeated 3000 Spaniards, and captured seven ships in the harbour of St. Jago de la Cuba; and eventually took the town and castle, with the cannon of the works, and five hundred barrels of powder. Not enjoying his health in that climate, his Lordship received permission to return to England; and, after his arrival, he was appointed one of his Majesty's Privy Council in Ireland. At length his Majesty, taking into consideration the eminent services of Lord Windsor, advanced him to the dignity of EARL OF PLYMOUTH, by patent dated the 6th of December, 1682.

The EARL OF PLYMOUTH enjoyed the affection and confidence of King James II., who conferred upon him the Colonelcy of the FOURTH REGIMENT OF HORSE (now 3rd Dragoon Guards), and also appointed him one of the Privy Council. He died on the 3rd of November, 1687, and was buried in the church of Tarbick.

SIR JOHN FENWICK, BART.,

Appointed 6th November, 1687.

JOHN FENWICK, Esq., was a loyal cavalier in the reign of King Charles II., and an officer of the Queen's Troop (now Second Regiment) of Life Guards. He served under the Duke of

Monmouth, with the French army, in the Netherlands, during the campaigns of 1672 and 1673. In the succeeding year he obtained permission to proceed to Holland; and, in 1675, he was appointed Colonel of an Irish regiment in the Dutch service (the present Fifth Foot). He served with his regiment during the campaign of that year under the Prince of Orange; and, in the following summer, he served at the siege of Maestricht, where he was severely wounded while on duty with his regiment in the trenches (2nd August, 1676). Shortly afterwards some angry words passed between him and the Prince of Orange, when he quitted the Dutch service, and, returning to England, resumed his duties in the Life Guards; and, from this period, a personal aversion is said to have existed between his Highness and Colonel Fenwick. The Colonel was, however, well received at the British court: he succeeded, on the decease of his father, to the dignity of a baronet, and, in 1678, King Charles II. promoted him to the rank of Brigadier-General, and gave him the Colonelcy of a newly-raised regiment of foot, with which he proceeded to Flanders; but, after the peace of Nimeguen, this regiment was disbanded, and Sir John again resumed his duties in the Life Guards, in which corps he rose to the rank of Lieutenant and Lieutenant-Colonel. In 1686 he was appointed Inspecting General of Cavalry (jointly with Brigadier-General Sir John Lanier), and, after the decease of the Earl of Plymouth in 1687, he was promoted from the Life Guards to the Colonelcy of the FOURTH HORSE. He was also Governor of Holy Island, and a Member of Parliament for the county of Northumberland.

Sir John Fenwick appears to have been devotedly attached to the Stuart dynasty; and, having been advanced to the rank of Major-General in November, 1688, he refused to take the required oath to the Prince of Orange at the Revolution, and his regiment was given to Viscount Colchester. After the accession of William and Mary, Sir John did not abstain from corresponding with the dethroned monarch. After the decease of Queen Mary, he assisted in planning an insurrection in favour of King James, which was to have broken out in the winter of 1695-6, and he agreed to command a body of horse. At this time a plot for the assassination of King William was discovered, and Sir John Fenwick was apprehended at New Romney, on his way to France, on an attainder of high treason, and was brought to trial before the Parliament. No proof of his guilt was produced; but the written evidence of a witness on a former trial was produced against him. This proceeding gave rise to much altercation amongst the members; but the Bill was at length carried by a majority of seven: forty-one Lords, including eight Prelates, entering a protest against the decision. An offer of pardon was made to him by the Peers, on condition that he would make a full discovery; but he chose to suffer death rather than incur the disgrace of becoming an informer. He was beheaded on Tower Hill on the 28th of January, 1697. At the time of his execution, he professed his attachment to King James, and expressed a wish that the exiled monarch might be restored to the throne.

RICHARD VISCOUNT COLCHESTER,

Appointed 31st December, 1688.

This nobleman entered the Life Guards, in which corps he attained, in the spring of 1686, the rank of Lieutenant and Lieutenant-Colonel. He was one of the first officers who joined the Prince of Orange at the Revolution in 1688, and he took with him several private gentlemen of the fourth troop of Life Guards. On the removal of Sir John Fenwick, the Colonelcy of the FOURTH REGIMENT OF HORSE was conferred on Viscount Colchester, who attended King William in Ireland, and was at the battle of the Boyne and the siege of Limerick. His lordship was removed to the Colonelcy of the Third Troop of Life Guards in 1692, which gave him the privilege of taking the court duty of Gold Stick, and he served with distinction under his Majesty in several campaigns on the Continent. He succeeded to the title of EARL RIVERS in 1694; and, in the early campaigns of the wars of Queen Anne, he served under the celebrated John Duke of Marlborough. In 1706 he commanded an expedition designed to make a descent on the French coast; but the fleet having been delayed by contrary winds until the design was frustrated, he proceeded to Spain, where he left the troops under the command of the Earl of Galway, and afterwards returned to England. He was appointed to the Colonelcy of the Royal Horse Guards in 1712; and died in the same year.

JOHN LORD BERKELEY,

Appointed 23d January, 1692.

This nobleman was the son of Sir John Berkeley, a descendant from the ancient Barons of Berkeley Castle (and a distinguished loyalist in the time of Charles I. and Charles II.), who was raised to the peerage by the title of LORD BERKELEY, OF STRATTON. Having entered the Royal Navy, he rose to the rank of Admiral, and was also Colonel of a regiment of Marines (afterwards disbanded) in the reign of Charles II. It was common at this period for the Admirals to hold commissions in the army. After the Revolution of 1688, Lord Berkeley sustained a military character, and was appointed Colonel of the FOURTH REGIMENT OF HORSE in January, 1692. He, however, quitted the regiment in the following year, and held a naval command, in which he distinguished himself against the French. Lord Berkelcy died on the 29th of February, 1697.

CORNELIUS WOOD,

Appointed 24th January, 1694.

This officer was the son of a clergyman of Staffordshire, and having been unfortunate in commerce, in the reign of Charles II., he entered Queen Catherine's Troop (now Second

Regiment) of Life Guards, as a private gentleman, at the time when the ranks of that corps contained many young men of distinction who were aspiring to commissions in the regular army. Mr. Wood evinced great attention in acquiring a knowledge of his profession, which, with a strict performance of all his duties, soon procured him the approbation and favour of Sir Philip Howard, the Captain and Colonel, and of Sir George Hewytt, the Lieutenant-Colonel, through whose recommendation he was advanced to the post of Sub-Corporal with the rank of Cornet; and, on the 15th of June, 1685, King James II. promoted him to the degree of Corporal (or Brigadier) with the rank of Lieutenant. During the remainder of the short reign of James II., Brigadier Wood is said to have witnessed with regret the violent conduct of the King; and, being faithful to the principles which he had imbibed in his youth, he adhered to the Protestant interest at the Revolution in 1688, and was promoted, by King William III., to the Captaincy of a troop in the Ninth Horse (now Sixth Dragoon Guards), the command of which corps had been conferred on his friend, Sir George Hewytt, afterwards Viscount Hewytt. The intrepidity which he displayed in the wars in Ireland and in Flanders[59] gained him a high reputation, and he was promoted to the Lieutenant-Colonelcy of the regiment on the 31st of December, 1692. His gallant conduct at the battle of Landen, on the 19th of July, 1693, attracted the attention of King William, who complimented him on his bravery, made him a present of a valuable charger, and, in January of the following year,[119] His Majesty promoted him to the Colonelcy of the FOURTH HORSE; at the head of which regiment he served in Flanders until the peace of Ryswick in 1697.

On the breaking out of the war in 1702, Colonel Wood was promoted to the rank of Brigadier-General, and sent with his regiment to Holland, to serve under the celebrated John Duke of Marlborough; and, in the following year, he was advanced to the rank of Major-General. The several campaigns of this war form a glorious era in the military history of Great Britain; and few officers acquired greater celebrity than General Wood. In the annals of that war his name is associated with exploits of particular brilliancy; and he is mentioned among those who materially contributed to the victories at Schellenberg, Blenheim, and Ramilies. At the latter engagement, the Duke of Bavaria and Marshal Villiers narrowly escaped being taken prisoners by him, as more particularly stated in the record of the Third Dragoon Guards. He also distinguished himself at the battle of Malplaquet, and in several skirmishes.

The death of this distinguished officer was occasioned by the fall of his horse in May, 1712.

Thomas Viscount Windsor,

Appointed 18th May, 1712.

Lord Thomas Windsor, second son of Thomas Earl of Plymouth, the first Colonel of this regiment, served with distinction in the army in the wars of King William III., and, on the 23rd of January, 1692, he obtained the Lieutenant-Colonelcy of the Fourth Horse. On the 16th of February, 1694, he was appointed to the Colonelcy of a newly-raised regiment of horse, which was disbanded after the peace of Ryswick. On the 19th of June, 1699, he was advanced to the peerage of Ireland by the title of Viscount Windsor. After the decease of the Earl of Macclesfield, in 1701, the Colonelcy of the Tenth Horse was conferred upon Viscount Windsor, who was promoted, on the 9th of March, 1702, to the rank of Brigadier-General,[120] and on 1st of January, 1704, to that of Major-General. In October of the latter year his regiment was given to Samuel (afterwards Lord) Masham. The rank of Lieutenant-General was, however, conferred upon his Lordship in 1707; in April, 1711, he was restored to the Colonelcy of the Tenth Horse; and in December of the same year, he was made an English Peer, by the title of Baron Montjoy, of the Isle of Wight. The Colonelcy of the Fourth Horse was conferred upon his Lordship in 1712; from which he was removed, by King George I., in 1717: he died in 1738.

George Wade,

Appointed 19th March, 1717.

This officer engaged in the profession of arms in the reign of William III., and, after serving the Crown with zeal and fidelity for many years, he was eventually rewarded with the highest honours of the service. His first commission was dated the 26th of December, 1690; and he served in the Netherlands under King William until the peace of Ryswick. Having rose to the rank of Lieutenant-Colonel of the Tenth Regiment of Foot, he proceeded, on the breaking out of the war of the Spanish succession, with the expedition to Portugal, and was appointed Adjutant-General to the army commanded by the Earl of Galway, with the brevet rank of Colonel, by commission dated the 22nd of August, 1704. After the death of Colonel Duncasson, who was killed at the siege of Valencia de Alcantara, in May, 1705, the command of the Thirty-third Foot was conferred upon Colonel Wade, by commission bearing date the 9th of June in the same year. Continuing to serve in the Peninsula, and, by his personal exertions, gaining laurels even in the midst of the reverses and disasters which befell the army, he was promoted to the rank of Brigadier-General on the 1st of January, 1708; and, in the following year he received a complimentary communication from King Charles III. (afterwards Emperor of the Romans), with the commission of Major-General in Spain; in which country he served during the remainder of the war, and highly distinguished himself in the command of a brigade of infantry at the battle of Saragossa in 1710.

On the accession of King George I., Brigadier-General Wade was advanced to the rank of Major-General; and, proving a faithful and trustworthy servant to the Crown, at a time when jacobin principles were prevalent in the nation, his Majesty appointed him, on the 19th of March, 1717, Colonel of the Fourth Horse. In 1724 he commanded in Scotland; and some important roads through the Highlands were constructed under his direction and superintendence.

He was promoted to the rank of Lieutenant-General on the 7th of March, 1727; to that of General on the 2nd of July, 1739; and he was further advanced to the rank of Field-Marshal on the 14th of December, 1743. In the following year, this distinguished veteran, being then in the seventy-sixth year of his age, engaged in active service, and commanded the British troops in the Netherlands in the campaign of 1744, but afterwards returned to England; and, in the succeeding year, he was appointed Commander-in-Chief, during the absence of his Royal Highness the Duke of Cumberland on the Continent. In the autumn of the same year a rebellion broke out in Scotland, and Field-Marshal Wade commanded an army in Yorkshire, and was actively engaged in the pursuit of the rebels after their retreat from Derby. He was Lieutenant-General of the Ordnance and one of his Majesty's Privy Council; and, after serving the Crown a period of fifty-eight years, died on the 14th of February, 1748, in the eightieth year of his age.

THE HON. SIR CHARLES HOWARD, K.B.,

Appointed 15th March, 1748.

THE HONOURABLE CHARLES HOWARD, second son of Charles third Earl of Carlisle, entered the army in the second year of the reign of King George I., and was appointed Captain and Lieutenant-Colonel in the Coldstream Guards in April, 1719. He was appointed Deputy-Governor of Carlisle in March, 1725; rose to the rank of Colonel on the 23rd of April, 1734; and was appointed Aide-de-camp to King George II. He was promoted, on the 1st of November, 1738, to the command of the Nineteenth Regiment of Foot; was appointed Brigadier-General on the 18th of February, 1742, and proceeded with the army, commanded by the Earl of Stair, to Flanders, in the same year. He was promoted to the rank of Major-General on the 4th of July, 1743; to that of Lieutenant-General on thc 9th of August, 1747; and, in March, 1748, to the Colonelcy of the THIRD DRAGOON GUARDS. In June, 1749, he was created a Knight of the most honourable Order of the

Bath; and, in March, 1765, he was promoted to the rank of General.

SIR CHARLES HOWARD was Governor of Forts George and Augustus in Scotland; one of the Grooms of the Bedchamber; and was many years a Member of Parliament for the city of Carlisle, of which he was Lieutenant-Governor; and died on the 26th of August, 1765.

LORD ROBERT MANNERS,

Appointed 6th September, 1765.

LORD ROBERT MANNERS, son of John second Duke of Rutland, choosing a military life, purchased an Ensigncy in the Coldstream Guards on the 26th of July, 1735; was appointed Lieutenant in May, 1740; and Captain and Lieutenant-Colonel in the First Foot Guards on the 22nd of April, 1742. In December, 1747, he was promoted to the rank of Colonel, and appointed Aide-de-camp to King George II.; and, in 1751, his Majesty gave him the Colonelcy of the Thirty-sixth Regiment of Foot. The rank of Major-General was conferred upon Lord Robert Manners on the 7th of February, 1757; that of Lieutenant-General on the 7th of April, 1759; and, in 1765, King George III. gave him the Colonelcy of the THIRD DRAGOON GUARDS, with the rank of General, five years afterwards: he died on the 31st of May, 1782.

PHILIP HONEYWOOD,

Appointed 7th June, 1782.

PHILIP HONEYWOOD, having entered the army at an early age, rose to the rank of Major in the King's Dragoons, now Third Light Dragoons, with which corps he proceeded to Flanders in 1742, and displayed great gallantry at the battle of Dettingen on the 26th of June, 1743, where his regiment was warmly engaged with the French household troops and suffered severely. Major Honeywood received five wounds in this action, and, being thought dead, he was stripped by some plunderers, and lay in that state six hours on the field of battle. He, however, revived, and, having recovered of his wounds, resumed his regimental duties, and was at the battle of Fontenoy on the 11th of May, 1745. In the autumn of the same year the rebellion broke out in Scotland, when the King's Dragoons were ordered to return to England; and, on the flight of the rebels from Derby, the regiment, being sent forward in pursuit, overtook the rear-guard on Clifton Moor, in Lancashire, on the 19th of December, and a sharp action ensuing, Lieutenant-Colonel Honeywood again displayed his wonted bravery, and was severely wounded in the shoulder. He, however, recovered; and, on the 17th of March, 1752, was promoted to the rank of Colonel in the army; and, in April, 1755, King George II. gave him the Colonelcy of the Twentieth Regiment of Foot; from which he was removed, in May of the following year, to the Ninth Dragoons. He was promoted to the rank of Major-General on the 17th of May, 1758; and, on the 5th of April in the following year, he obtained the Colonelcy of the Fourth Irish Horse, now the Seventh Dragoon Guards.

During the Seven Years' War, Major-General Honeywood commanded a brigade of cavalry in Germany under Prince Ferdinand of Brunswick, and performed a distinguished part in many skirmishes and general engagements; particularly at the battle of Warbourg, on the 31st of July, 1760, when he led his own regiment to the charge with signal gallantry: the enemy was overthrown, the most dreadful slaughter followed, and many of the French were drowned in attempting to escape across the river Dymel. In December of the same year he was promoted to the rank of Lieutenant-General; and, continuing to serve in Germany, he acquired great celebrity, and was commended by the Commander-in-Chief in his public despatches. After his return to England he was advanced to the rank of General; and a vacancy occurring in the Colonelcy of the THIRD DRAGOON GUARDS, in 1782, King George III. conferred that appointment on this distinguished veteran.

General Honeywood was many years Governor of Hull; he was also Member of Parliament for Appleby; and died on the 20th of January, 1785.

RICHARD BURTON PHILIPSON,

Appointed 23rd February, 1785.

RICHARD BURTON commenced his military service in the reign of King George II.; and, having attained the rank of Major in the Royal Dragoons on the 1st of May, 1759, proceeded with his regiment to Germany in the spring of the following year. In the battles, skirmishes, fatigues, and privations of the three subsequent campaigns, MAJOR BURTON had his share; as well as in the honours acquired by the British cavalry. After his return to England he was permitted to take the surname of PHILIPSON. On the 25th of January, 1771, he was appointed Lieutenant-Colonel of the Royal Dragoons; and, in 1775, he was appointed Colonel in the army and Aide-de-camp to King George III. On the breaking out of the American war, several new regiments were raised, and Colonel Philipson was promoted to the rank of Major-General, and appointed Colonel of the Twentieth Light Dragoons (a corps formed of the light troops of several other regiments), on the 25th of April, 1779; from which he was removed, on the 23rd of February, 1785, to the THIRD DRAGOON GUARDS. He was promoted to the rank of Lieutenant-General on the 28th of September, 1787; was Member of Parliament for Eye, in Suffolk; and died on the 19th of August, 1792.

SIR WILLIAM FAWCETT, K.B.,

Appointed 22nd August, 1792.

WILLIAM FAWCETT, who descended from the ancient family of Fawcetts, of Shipden Hall, near Halifax, having, from his early youth, a strong predilection for a military life, his friends procured him an Ensign's commission in General Oglethorp's regiment, which was stationed in Georgia; but, a

British force having been sent to Flanders in 1742, he resigned his commission, proceeded to the Continent, and, serving as a volunteer, was at the battles of Dettingen and Fontenoy, where his gallantry attracted admiration; and he was appointed Ensign in a regiment raised by Colonel Johnstone, with which he served until the peace of Aix-la-Chapelle, in 1748, when it was disbanded.

Being now unemployed, he engaged in the service of a mercantile establishment in the city of London; but, finding his propensity to a military life invincible, he subsequently purchased an Ensign's commission in the Foot Guards, and, by a strict attention to his duties, procured the favour of his Royal Highness William Duke of Cumberland, who gave him the Adjutantcy of the second battalion of the Third Foot Guards, which he held, together with a Lieutenantcy, which gave him the rank of Captain. Neglecting no opportunity of qualifying himself for the highest posts in his profession, he studied the German and French languages, acquired a knowledge of Prussian and French tactics; and, in 1757, published a translation of the 'Memoirs upon the Art of War, by Marshal Count de Saxe,' and 'The Regulations for the Prussian Cavalry;' and, in 1759, 'The Regulations for the Prussian Infantry,' and 'The Prussian Tactics.' These works met with great attention; and a new edition in 1760 was also well received.

In the early part of the Seven Years' War, Captain Fawcett served in Germany as Aide-de-camp to Lieutenant-General Grenville Elliott, where he acquired a practical knowledge of the military art; and his ardour, intrepidity, and attention to the duties of his situation were such, that, on the decease of Lieutenant-General Grenville Elliott, Captain Fawcett was recommended for the appointment of Aide-de-camp to Prince Ferdinand of Brunswick, and he had also the offer of the same appointment to the Marquis of Granby: he chose the latter, and was sent to England with the despatches which gave the account of the victory at Warbourg; on which occasion, King George II. was highly gratified at having the particulars of this engagement related to him in the German language by Captain Fawcett. He was advanced to the rank of Lieutenant-Colonel in the army on the 25th of November, 1760; and, continuing to serve in Germany, was appointed Military Secretary to the Marquis of Granby. It is recorded that, in Lieutenant-Colonel Fawcett's character, strength and softness were happily blended together, and to coolness, intrepidity, and extensive military knowledge, he added all the requisite talents of a man of business, and the most persevering assiduity. He was highly esteemed by every officer on the staff of the army, and was the intimate and confidential friend of the Marquis of Granby. He remained on service until the peace in 1763, when he returned to England; and his knowledge of the German language, with the information he possessed from his late office, was the occasion of his being employed by King George III. as Commissary to settle the claims made by the Allies against Great Britain for the expenses of the war.

In November, 1767, he obtained a company in the Third Foot Guards; and, in 1772, he was promoted to the rank of Colonel in the army, and appointed Deputy Adjutant-General to the Forces.

At the commencement of the American war, Colonel Fawcett was sent to Germany to negotiate with the states of Hesse, Hanover, and Brunswick, for a body of troops to serve in North America, Gibraltar, and the East Indies. He was appointed Governor of Gravesend and Tilbury Fort on the 2nd of October, 1776. In 1777 he was promoted to the rank of Major-General; in the following year he was appointed Colonel of the Fifteenth Regiment of Foot; and, in 1781, he was appointed Adjutant-General to the Forces. The rank of Lieutenant-General was conferred upon this valuable servant of the Crown in 1782; in 1786 his Majesty honoured him with the riband of the Order of the Bath; and, in 1792, gave him the Colonelcy of THE THIRD, OR PRINCE OF WALES' DRAGOON GUARDS.

In May, 1796, Sir William Fawcett was promoted to the rank of General; and, in July following, he was appointed

Governor of the Royal Hospital at Chelsea. The office of Adjutant-General requiring greater exertions than his age would admit of, he obtained his Majesty's permission to resign, and, on retiring from his post, the King honoured him with distinguished marks of his Royal favour and approbation. In 1799 the Duke of York proceeded to Holland, when Sir William Fawcett was appointed by his Majesty to be *General on the Staff* of the Army, and to perform the duties of Commander-in-Chief during his Royal Highness's absence.

He died on the 19th of March, 1804; and his funeral was honoured with the presence of his Royal Highness the Prince of Wales, their Royal Highnesses the Dukes of York, Clarence, Kent, and Cambridge, and of many noblemen and General Officers.

RICHARD VYSE,

Appointed 2nd April, 1804.

GENERAL VYSE entered the army, on the 13th of February, 1762, as Cornet of the Fifth Royal Irish Dragoons; obtained the rank of Lieutenant in 1766; and, having become particularly proficient in the duties of his profession, was appointed Adjutant of the regiment in March of the following year. Having purchased a Captaincy in 1771, he procured the commission of Major in the Eighteenth Light Dragoons in 1777; and, in 1784, was appointed Lieutenant-Colonel of the King's Dragoon Guards, which corps he brought into a high state of discipline and efficiency; and was promoted to the rank of Colonel in the army in 1791. On the breaking out of the war with France, in 1793, he proceeded with his regiment on foreign service; and, in the following year, commanded a brigade of heavy cavalry under his Royal Highness the Duke of York, and distinguished himself on several occasions—particularly at the battle of Cateau, on the 26th of April, 1794, where, after the fall of Major-General Mansel, he commanded two brigades throughout the remainder of the day, and materially contributed to the victory gained on that occasion. In October of the same year he was promoted to the rank of Major-General; in 1797 his Majesty gave him the Colonelcy of the Twenty-ninth Dragoons; and, in 1801, promoted him to the rank of Lieutenant-General.

After the decease of Sir William Fawcett, the King conferred the Colonelcy of the PRINCE OF WALES' DRAGOON GUARDS on Lieutenant-General Vyse, who was advanced to the rank of General on the 1st of January, 1812; and died in 1825.

SIR WILLIAM PAYNE, BART.,

Appointed 2nd June, 1825.

SIR WILLIAM PAYNE first entered the army, as Cornet in the Royal Dragoons, on the 25th of January, 1776; and, having served in the subordinate commissions, was appointed Lieutenant-Colonel of the regiment in 1794. He served in the Netherlands under his Royal Highness the Duke of York, and was present at the principal actions during the campaign of 1794. In 1796 he was removed from the Lieutenant-Colonelcy of the Royal Dragoons to the THIRD DRAGOON GUARDS; in 1798 he was promoted to the rank of Colonel in the army; and, in 1805, he was removed to the Tenth Light Dragoons. He was promoted to the rank of Major-General in the same year, and served four years on the Staff in Ireland. In November, 1807, he obtained the Colonelcy of the Twenty-third Light Dragoons; and, in 1809, he proceeded to Portugal with the local rank of Lieutenant-General, and served the campaign of that year under Sir Arthur Wellesley. He took an active part in the operations by which the French were driven from Oporto; and commanded the British cavalry at the memorable battle of Talavera, fought on the 27th and 28th of July, 1809, for which he received a medal. He was promoted to the rank of Lieutenant-General on the 4th of June, 1811; was removed from the Twenty-third to the Nineteenth Light Dragoons in July, 1814, and to the Twelfth Lancers in January, 1815. He was further advanced to the rank of General on the 27th of May, 1825; and, in the following month, he obtained the Colonelcy of the THIRD DRAGOON GUARDS. He subsequently took the name of Galway; and died in April, 1831.

SAMUEL HAWKER, G.C.H.,

Appointed 22nd April, 1831.

FOOTNOTE:

[59] *Vide* the Historical Record of the Sixth Dragoon Guards.

www.ingramcontent.com/pod-product-compliance
Lightning Source LLC
LaVergne TN
LVHW010035160826
845671LV00004B/202

* 9 7 8 9 3 5 4 7 8 4 2 5 5 *